# PLAYING THE SCENE
# OF RELIGION

# PLAYING THE SCENE OF RELIGION

## BEAUVOIR AND FAITH

KAREN ELIZABETH ZOPPA

SHEFFIELD UK    BRISTOL CT

Published by Equinox Publishing Ltd.
UK:     Office 415, The Workstation, 15 Paternoster Row, Sheffield, South Yorkshire S1 2BX
USA:    ISD, 70 Enterprise Drive, Bristol, CT 06010

www.equinoxpub.com

First published 2021

© Karen Elizabeth Zoppa

All rights reserved. No part of this publication may be reproduced or transmitted in any form or by any means, electronic or mechanical, including photocopying, recording or any information storage or retrieval system, without prior permission in writing from the publishers.

British Library Cataloguing-in-Publication Data
A catalogue record for this book is available from the British Library.
ISBN-13   978 1 80050 061 7  (hardback)
          978 1 80050 062 4  (paperback)
          978 1 80050 063 1  (ePDF)
          978 1 80050 115 7  (ePub)

Library of Congress Cataloging-in-Publication Data

Names: Zoppa, Karen, author.
Title: Playing the scene of religion : Beauvoir and faith / by Karen Elizabeth Zoppa.
Description: Sheffield, South Yorkshire ; Bristol, CT : Equinox Publishing Ltd, 2021. | Includes bibliographical references and index. | Summary: "This book interrogates popular notions of religion by reading it, out of Derrida and Certeau, as a signifier for a situated historical scene, and shows the existential philosophy of Beauvoir as a performance of that scene"-- Provided by publisher.
Identifiers: LCCN 2021011535 (print) | LCCN 2021011536 (ebook) | ISBN 9781800500617 (hardback) | ISBN 9781800500624 (paperback) | ISBN 9781800500631 (epdf) | ISBN 9781800501157 (epub)
Subjects: LCSH: Beauvoir, Simone de, 1908-1986--Religion. | Derrida, Jacques. | Certeau, Michel de. | Religion--Philosophy.
Classification: LCC B2430.B344 Z67 2021  (print) | LCC B2430.B344  (ebook) | DDC 210--dc23
LC record available at https://lccn.loc.gov/2021011535
LC ebook record available at https://lccn.loc.gov/2021011536


Typeset by S.J.I. Services, New Delhi, India

# Contents

| | |
|---|---|
| Acknowledgements | vii |
| Introduction | 1 |
| Chapter 1<br>Writing Lives | 6 |
| Chapter 2<br>Setting the Scene | 23 |
| Chapter 3<br>Beauvoir's Conversion | 65 |
| Chapter 4<br>The Other Shore | 84 |
| Chapter 5<br>A Moving Scene | 116 |
| Bibliography | 124 |
| Index of Names and Select Titles by Author | 129 |
| Index of Subjects | 131 |

# Acknowledgements

I gratefully acknowledge the following: The University of Winnipeg for allowing me the time and resources to produce this book; the support and wisdom of my mentors, Dr. Elizabeth Alexandrin and Dr. Louise Renée of the University of Manitoba; and the astute editorial advice of Dr. Catherine Hunter of the University of Winnipeg. Above all, I must express my abiding gratitude and love to my family for their patience and humor.

I also acknowledge the permission granted to re-print material from the following:

*Acts of Religion* by Jacques Derrida, edited by Gil Andijar (Routledge, 2002). Reproduced by permission of Taylor & Francis Group.

*The Ethics of Ambiguity* by Simone de Beauvoir, translated by Bernard Frechtman (Citadel Press, 1948, 1976). Reproduced by permission of the Philosophical Library, New York.

*Pyrrhus and Cineas* by Simone de Beauvoir, from *Philosophical Writings*. Copyright 2005 Board of Trustees of the University of Illinois. Used with permission of the University of Illinois Press.

# Introduction

"'May I not be separated from thee.' Not without thee."
Michel de Certeau, *The Mystic Fable*[1]

The history of European civilization was once introduced to me by suggesting we examine the tallest buildings of its various eras: in the beginning, the tallest building was the temple or cathedral, the era of the rule of the priests; next, the tallest buildings were the castles and fortresses, the era of the rule of the princes; finally, in our own era, the tallest buildings are the towers of commerce, the era of the rule of the capitalists. In this view, ecclesia, aristocracy and capitalism are each organized according to a similar hierarchical design, a stratification of classes, an assertion of authority over apostasy. The story is, of course, a narrow over-simplification of the complex circulation of goods, ideas, practices, and people that are lumped into the category "European civilization." However, it contains a grain of truth: that the ruling institution in any given era may change its mode, but not its operation. In a way, one can draw a direct line from Constantine's Holy Roman Empire to the global capitalist G7 of today. The authority of God has been replaced by Mammon, but the structure and its mechanisms remain the same.

I invoke this fable because it supplies an entreé into the matter of this study: reading religion as the performative structure in this long, amorphous story of Europe, a structure that produces strange contradictions, specifically, the necessity of faith in the existential philosophy of Simone de Beauvoir.

---

1 Michel de Certeau, *The Mystic Fable* (Chicago: University of Chicago Press, 1986), 1.

Simone de Beauvoir is an atheist in the most pristine sense, dismissing both the god of her Roman Catholic tradition and the metaphysics that underwrite it. "He had ceased to exist for me,"[2] she recalls, as she becomes liberated into her own experience of the world as the guiding source for her life. At the same time, freed from an unattainable and unkowable heaven, she discovers herself "condemned to death,"[3] the necessary condition for the development of her existential philosophy. Her autobiography details her own strict, deeply pious Catholic girlhood and her subsequent rejection of that tradition. When Beauvoir dismisses God as a viable concept, as well as the Roman Catholic prescriptions for bourgeois French women, it is assumed that she has clearly rejected religion. However, her writings, continuously testifying to her own "useless passion" for an impossible "absolute," witness her journey to understand this endless desire, and its implication for how to live a meaningful life.

The claim that she had moved away from religion is founded on popular notions of religion that insist it is something that involves God, beliefs in metaphysical claims, and prescribed practices within some institutional framework. This study approaches "religion" not as some discrete category of human behaviour, but instead as the deep mechanism governing European and now global capitalist society for the past 2,000 years. According to this reading, religion is the inescapable and necessary architecture of Beauvoir's project. Within this structure, Beauvoir's philosophy can be seen as a movement of that same machinery I am calling the scene of religion, restrained by and exceeding the metaphysical enclosure of the European tradition.

This study has two agendas: to interrogate popular notions of religion by reading it as a signifier for a situated historical scene; and to show the existential philosophy of Beauvoir as a performance of that scene. In particular, it will show how the structure of relationships she presents in her ethics clearly reproduces the rhythms of the scene of religion. One of the implications of this reproduction is that existential philosophy can only emerge in the context of religion. Another implication is that we must reassess how we code the category religion in our public and private discourse.

What is the scene of religion? At present, much of the study of religion in academia is concerned with the problem of defining religion, from within a variety of functional and critical perspectives. For reasons given more fully in subsequent chapters, I am reading religion in specific texts

---

2 Simone de Beauvoir, *Memoirs of a Dutiful Daughter* (New York: Harper Perennial Modern Classics, 2003), 137.
3 Beauvoir, *Memoirs of a Dutiful Daughter*, 138.

by Jacques Derrida, a reading magnified in a study by Michel de Certeau, in order to understand the tropes of religion in Beauvoir. This theoretical commitment requires spending some time constructing an accessible *theoria* from Derrida's prolific writings on religion. It is also necessary to spend some time looking at a situated example of the scene religion in Certeau. Such a review will literally set the scene in which to examine Beauvoir's ethic as an iteration of religion.

This "scene of religion" is the play of authority and resistance, orthodoxy and heresy, replicated and reproduced throughout Europe and, by extension, its colonial outposts. I am proposing, following Derrida, that this scene is the culmination of those impulses toward identity, unity and totalization, often "in the name of the Father, the Son and the Holy," that gather in the Greek and Roman worlds, and rise and fall in momentum in the institutions of Christianity. These impulses continue to evolve into the present techno-liberal capitalist economic and political hegemony of our contemporary world, wherein demands for social and political conformity are always already undone by the play of teeming heterogeneous forces. Exhibiting a logic of *différance*, the machinery that reproduces this scene involves a binary of resistance that creates and dismantles identities, a binary that Derrida says is founded in "faith" and "knowledge" in a play of autoimmunity.[4] In this play, I promise to protect, preserve and indemnify a certain knowledge and its power in response to an other, who has promised me they offer truth, even though they may be lying or may fail to keep their promise. One appeals and the other responds, both reproducing the truth they indemnify and protect. At the same time, the response produces resistance against that which threatens it, a thrusting out which ironically reproduces the very disturbance that the move to indemnify seeks to prevent. Beauvoir and her *Ethics of Ambiguity* are an instance of this resistance. The desire that drives this play is also the desire which opens into faith, the response to the other that she claims founds the meaning of our lives.

Where Derrida reveals the machinery of religion in a number of texts, Certeau offers a detailed examination of this play, the history of the mystic turn of the 16th and 17th centuries, a moment that can be seen as the prologue to the present economic and political hegemony. The mystics of 16th and 17th century Europe rebel against a dogma and orthodoxy that ceases to speak to them the living word of the One who is absent. Their resistance takes the form of a "manner of speaking," which is itself a performance of

---

4 Jacques Derrida, "Faith and Knowledge: The Sources of Religion at the Limit of Reason Alone." *Acts of Religion*, edited by Gil Andijar (New York: Routledge, 2002), 79–80.

a kind of faith, a commitment to communicate that which is absent, a commitment which must be expressed heterogeneously. A consequence of this mystic turn is the failure of the mystics to restore the absent "Body" of the One, either in the Church "faithful," or in scriptural exegesis, or in history. They are doomed to wander in search of that absence, and to identify only that which is not the One, a *via negativa*. At the same time, the institutions of European Christianity push back against the mystic incursion on their hegemony and, in the process, incorporate the mystic forms, if not their spirit. These tropes of the mystic discourse are then subject to the same play of indemnification and resistance, a play which produces the iterations that constitute the social and political context of Beauvoir's life: the bourgeois French Catholic milieu of the early 20th century.

I read Beauvoir as the heir to this post–mystic iteration of the Catholic Church, a Church which saw the surrender of its power to the emerging economic and political matrix of the modern state, even as it functions to enable that state. She also inherits the self-as-subject, freighted with the Enlightenment's focus on the autonomy of the rational self, especially from Kant and Hegel. Beauvoir's philosophical reflections lead her to the figure of ambiguity, which acknowledges, among other things, that a human is both singular subject and at the same time social object, and that meaning can only ever arrive for the individual through her engagement with others.

The particular iteration of the scene of religion that manifests in Beauvoir's writing exhibits an unending desire for union with an "other,"[5] at the same time that her philosophy asserts the impossibility of any absolutes. In this, her philosophy engages that one source of religion, "faith," which always exceeds any determinate tradition. She enjoins us to an act of faith with the other that, contingent and fraught with risk, is the condition for any relationship. Like the Mystics of the 16th and 17th century that Certeau situates, Beauvoir resists a Word, an institution, a practice that no longer speaks truth, while struggling to discover, through her discourse, a regime that can.

In locating Beauvoir in the scene of religion revealed in Derrida and Certeau, we face a double injunction: on the one hand, her own texts and especially her ethic are subject to the very logic of *différance* that deconstruction reads; on the other hand, Beauvoir exhibits an awareness of and

---

5 Throughout this discussion, I will frequently refer to the philosophical concept of the "other," sometimes in lower case, sometimes in upper case, and sometimes within quotations marks, following its treatment by the author in question.

sensitivity to the aporetic in her existential philosophy, an awareness of an ambiguity that exceeds the machinery of autoimmunity. My reading of Beauvoir's ethic intends to show that the play in the scene of religion – the call of and response to the other – moves in the philosophy of an existential atheist, a philosophical position that is necessarily a response to the assumptions of European metaphysics. This movement in Beauvoir's philosophy enjoins a re-thinking of "religion" as it is commonly deployed as a category, and especially its use in the critique of contemporary social and political conflicts.

In the opening pages of *The Mystic Fable*, Michel de Certeau quotes the medieval Christian prayer, the *Anima Christi*: "*May I not be separated from thee.*"[6] In the ancient prayer, the antecedent for the pronoun "thee" is the divine being; for Certeau, in *The Mystic Fable*, the antecedent is the-One-who-is-missing, the Other that drives desire in the mystic discourse. Certeau's text remains ambivalent regarding the "identity" of the One, here pointing toward the historic empty tomb in Jerusalem, there implying the One as cipher for *tout autres*. Perhaps this is a fitting epitaph for this study and a figure that can assist us in thinking together "Beauvoir" and the "scene of religion." Beauvoir's philosophical ethic takes as its axiom that we live in a world that no longer offers a unified order of meaning, but that we can make our own meaning. However, meaning can only be located in relationships, with "others." "Not without thee" in the context of Beauvoir's philosophy expresses that axiom – that there is no meaning, "without thee," without the other to whom we respond in risk and faith. "Naught, without thee" might be an existential iteration of the ancient prayer. Beauvoir's considered reflections upon the Other, the failure of European metaphysics, the erosion of the traditional authorities, and the implications of the ambiguity of human existence produce *The Ethics of Ambiguity*, necessarily located in the scene of religion. Such a reading of "religion" enjoins a re-thinking of its common use as a category in public discourse, a re-visioning that may open the precincts of recognition in an increasingly plural world.

---

6 Certeau, *The Mystic Fable*, 1.

## Chapter 1

## Writing Lives

An introduction to the personal and intellectual biographies of the three principals in this discourse will enable those who are not familiar with Beauvoir to attain some sense of her significance, while offering readers of Beauvoir a context and apology for choosing Derrida and Certeau as architects for its theory.

Beauvoir is famous for her lifelong association with the philosopher Jean Paul Sartre, and for her monumental treatise on the status of women, *The Second Sex*. An icon of the French existential philosophy movement,[1] Beauvoir was a public intellectual who consistently avowed her atheism and dedication to individual autonomy, through her literary works, her editorial activity at *Les Temps Moderne*, and in her political causes. She was born to a deeply bourgeoise family of petty aristocrats and educated in the French Roman Catholic tradition of the early 20th century. The rigidity of the social conventions of her class and the demand for young Beauvoir to conform helps situate and make comprehensible her rejection of those norms, even as inescapable aspects of that same culture provide the structure for her existential philosophy.

Although Beauvoir is well-known for her atheism, she is rarely discussed in relation to "religion," and when she is, the discussion tends to assume, unlike this study, that "religion" is a self-evident discrete category of human activity.[2] A review of Beauvoir's biography and social context will

---

1   Sarah Bakewell, *At the Existential Cafe* (Toronto: Alfred A. Knopf Canada, 2016) offers an accessible social history of the era, in which Beauvoir is the only woman philosopher amongst the "mandarins" of the age.
2   Of the very few studies that consider Beauvoir and "religion," Amy Hollywood's *Sensible Ecstasies*, examines Beauvoir's personal and philosophical reflections

show that the French bourgeois culture of *la belle époque*, a culture ordered by the Roman Catholic apparatus and its pious followers, is itself an iteration of the play of forces that is "religion," ones that Beauvoir resists, transcends and translates. This claim will be developed and defended in Chapter Two. For now, I want to emphasize in Beauvoir's early life the influences of those forces which compel conformity while undermining that same drive, producing resistance and disruption: the Church; its puritan social code; the rigid conventions of the bourgeois class; and its fear of difference. All of these elements necessarily play into Beauvoir's philosophical investigations, constituting the context of her thought as well as the conditions for her resistance.

Simone Ernestine Lucie Marie Bertrand de Beauvoir was born in Paris on January 9, 1908, to a petty aristocratic bourgeois family, to a "world of propriety and "cultivated distinction," an artificial politeness that regulated every aspect of her family's lives and set them apart from the great body of French society,"[3] according to her biographer Deirdre Bair. Even as young as four years old, Beauvoir was expected to present her own embossed calling card when visiting, and then to remain in silent dignity throughout the visit, replicating the adults she was born to emulate,[4] behaviour she quickly learned to challenge. Her father, Georges Bertrand de Beauvoir from Limousin, and her mother, Francois Brasseur from the north-eastern region, belonged to the same economic class, that of government department officials and bankers, and they expected their offspring to marry one another in ways mutually beneficial to the wealth and status of each family. The Bertrand de Beauvoir family considered themselves "of minor nobility," tracing their family lineage to Guillaume de Champeaux in the year 1100, one of the founders of the University of Paris and a "luminary" of the Latin church.[5] Beauvoir's father, Georges, was the second son and youngest child of his father Ernest-Narcisse, and therefore did not stand to inherit the greatest part of his family's estate. A strikingly handsome man,

---

    on "the mystic," but Hollywood never interrogates mysticism or the broader category of religion. Joseph Mahon's *Simone de Beauvoir and Her Catholicism* does an exhaustive review of Beauvoir's persistent use of Roman Catholic language and Christian themes and allusions, in order to support the theses that she is a "luminously Catholic writer" (2), going so far as to say she is a theist, but simply not conscious of it. Mahon does not interrogate the category "religion" or the play of the Roman Catholic tradition within it.

3  Bair, *Simone de Beauvoir*, 12.
4  Bair, *Simone de Beauvoir*, 11.
5  Bair, *Simone de Beauvoir*, 12.

gifted intellectually, his love of scholarship was only matched by his love of performing. After the early death of his mother, he began to neglect his studies and disregard the Catholicism that shaped their family life before her death. As Bair observes, like his own father and most men of his class, he was a "skeptical believer" who eventually became a "cynical and vocal non-believer," while his mother and, later, his wife were responsible for the "actual observances" required for the proper appearances of their class.[6] This obvious hypocrisy was not regarded as unusual among the bourgeoisie, as long as one avoided "scandal," especially of the financial kind. Transgressions of the paternal flesh were overlooked as long as the wives and mothers protected the appearances of piety and good manners.

Although his father, Ernest-Narcisse, through his inheritance and his own hard work, was able to retire and enjoy his lavish Parisian home and estate at Meyrigniac, he did not bequeath Georges an income ample enough for him to live on comfortably, and encouraged him to seek a profession. Georges' love of performance led him to law, but he was never really interested in it: "he cared so little for success" in this profession that he did not bother to complete his thesis presentation, and became a secretary to a lawyer rather than practice himself.[7] Only when he was not received in the "best circles," possibly because he had not enough income to guarantee he was not a gold-digger to their marriageable daughters, did he finally become a practicing lawyer, although he continued to frequent the music halls and theatres at night. Charming, intelligent, elegant, eventually Georges' father "decided it was time for him to marry," and the "powerful marriage broking networks" of their social class[8] found him a suitable partner in Françoise Brasseur.

Françoise' family was "richer and more successful" than the Beauvoirs, but instead of emulating the aristocracy, as Ernest-Narcisse did, they held fast to "the traditional values, beliefs and behaviors of the bourgeoisie."[9] Françoise' mother, Lucie, had been raised in a convent with a "reverence for order and authority" that equaled that of her husband, Gustave Brasseur. The first-born child of Lucie and Gustave, Françoise was made to know all her life how disappointed her parents were that she was not born a boy. An intelligent and studious child, she was, like her mother, educated in a convent where she experienced the only real affection she

---

6 Bair, *Simone de Beauvoir*, 25.
7 Bair, *Simone de Beauvoir*, 27.
8 Bair, *Simone de Beauvoir*, 27.
9 Bair, *Simone de Beauvoir*, 27.

had ever known from the mother superior, "Mother Bertrand."[10] When she later timidly suggested to her own mother that she might like to become a nun, she was briskly reminded of her destiny: "to marry well to increase the family's wealth and standing."[11]

The superior wealth and success of the Brasseur family was not destined to last. Gustave Brasseur was disgraced as a schemer who had lost most of his own money and that of investors at the Bank of Meuse in Verdun, which he had started. Eventually sent to prison for 13 months, his scandalous actions did not discourage him from selling absurd investment schemes for the rest of his life. Understandably, he never did pay the lavish dowry promised to Georges when he married Françoise, sealing the financial fate of his daughter's family.[12] From a large beautiful apartment on the Boulevard de Montparnasse, by the summer of 1919, the family was forced to move to a much smaller 5th floor walk-up at the Rue de Rennes, largely because Georges gave up the law and drifted aimlessly from one part time position to another, while the crash after the war decimated his invested inheritance.[13]

Françoise Brasseur was, despite her wealthy upbringing, up to the challenge. In love with Georges, supported by him as the head of domestic affairs, she learned to manage the family's ever dwindling income with discipline and grace: "she had an integrity that was probably formed in her convent years and that was constantly reinforced by her steadfast devotion to her Church."[14] Baptizing both her daughters in the Catholic faith, "her devotion to the spiritual and her belief in the wisdom of the Church" stood in stark contrast to Georges, who "viewed the entire world with the detachment of a non-believer."[15] During the idyllic years on the Rue de Montparnasse, young Simone de Beauvoir was thoroughly indoctrinated in the social conventions of her class, and this was reinforced by her attendance at the prestigious if pedagogically inadequate Cours Adeline Désir.[16] Early on, the paradigm of Beauvoir's experience was firmly established: her devout, dutiful mother taught her social discipline, unselfishness and austerity, inculcating in her a reverence for the Church; her father's

---

10  Bair, *Simone de Beauvoir*, 28.
11  Bair, *Simone de Beauvoir*.
12  Bair, *Simone de Beauvoir*, 29.
13  Bair, *Simone de Beauvoir*, 50.
14  Bair, *Simone de Beauvoir*, 31.
15  Bair, *Simone de Beauvoir*, 36.
16  Bair, *Simone de Beauvoir*, 43.

intelligent and quiet unbelieving was presented as "natural." The effect was, according to Beauvoir's own account, that

> my father's individualism and pagan ethical standards were in complete contrast to the rigidly moral conventionalism of my mother's teaching. This imbalance, which made my life a kind of endless disputation, is the main reason I became an intellectual.[17]

This "imbalance" is also reflected in what eventually becomes her material circumstances: the haute bourgeois family who lives in poverty; the sisters Beauvoir, with their impeccable manners, so shabbily dressed; the idyllic summers spent at the wealthier family member's estates, only to return to the grim apartment on the Rue de Rennes: Beauvoir's childhood and youth are marked by a social, economic and intellectual ambiguity that will inform the structure of her thought, and perhaps explain her rebellion against such a rigidly coded and stratified social sphere. She recalls, "brought up as I was on convent morals and paternal nationalism, I was always getting bogged down in contradictions,"[18] for example, that "the man chosen by God to be his representative on earth had not to concern himself with earthly things."[19]

Inheriting both great intelligence and intellectual discipline from her parents, Simone de Beauvoir was encouraged from an early age, perhaps 10 or 11, to become educated, as she would never have a dowry and would have to support herself.[20] This suited her well, as she had already begun to see her own future as an intellectual.

Young Simone was a brilliant student, almost always at the top of her class, she passed her *baccalaureate* with distinction. By the time she was 17 years old, she turned her attention to obtaining credentials to become a teacher of philosophy, a position only recently opened up to women, and one that guaranteed an income and pension. Studying at the Sorbonne, she attained her first degree with honors, coming in second only to Simone Weil, followed by her friend Maurice Merleau Ponty in third place.[21] Her success galvanized her determination and in 1929, she was the youngest person ever to pass the demanding *agrégation* examination in philosophy, attaining second place to Sartre, possibly because the idea of awarding

---

17  Beauvoir, *Memoirs of a Dutiful Daughter*, 41.
18  Beauvoir, *Memoirs*, 32.
19  Beauvoir, *Memoirs*, 32.
20  Bair, *Simone de Beauvoir*, 57.
21  Bair, *Simone de Beauvoir*, 122.

a first to a woman was unthinkable.[22] For the next decade, employed as a *lycée* teacher for the French state, she developed her relationship with Sartre and the collection of friends known as the "family." She forged an avant garde and, for such a proper bourgeois woman, radical way of life that included an open relationship with Sartre, a refusal to perform domestic duties or seek material wealth, and an insistence on being taken seriously as an intellectual.[23]

During the decade leading up to the war, she pursued her dream of becoming a writer, producing an unpublished collection of loosely related short stories, *When Things of the Spirit Come First*, and drafting the earliest version of *L'Invitée*. During this period, she began to read Hussurl seriously, adopting his phenomenological strategy, and later, while Sartre was a prisoner of war, she took up Hegel – in German – as a distraction from the privations and anxieties of the German occupation. By the end of the war, she and Sartre had also made their way into Heidegger, whose *Being and Time* clearly influenced Sartre's *Being and Nothingness*.[24] It was during this period that she and Sartre befriended Albert Camus, who, along with Merleau-Ponty, launched the intellectual journal, *Les Temps Modernes*, at the end of the war.

Between 1938 and 1949, Beauvoir published three novels, two major philosophical essays, a monumental study of the status of women and one play, a staggering achievement in just over one decade. The 1943 novel *L'Invitee (She Came to Stay)* was enthusiastically received, followed by another stunning success in 1945 with *Les Sang des Autres (The Blood of Others)*. Her 1944 essay "Pyrrhus and Cinéas" was also well received. This success perhaps led Camus, by whom Beauvoir initially felt mocked, to ask her to write

22   Bair, *Simone de Beauvoir*, 145–46.
23   These details of Beauvoir's "essential" yet contingent relationship with Sartre, including her several long term love affairs with the American writer Nelson Algren, and later the French filmmaker, Claude Lanzman, are available in Beauvoir's autobiography, *The Prime of Life, Force of Circumstance: I* and *II*; *Wartime Diary*; *America Day by Day*, and *Letters from Sartre*. The recent publication of *Diary of a Philosophy Student I and II* also testifies to her early bi-sexuality, an item of intense speculation before these texts were available.
24   Beauvoir does not tell us precisely when she began to read Heidegger, although she remarks on her conversations about him with Sartre, see Beauvoir, *The Prime of Life*, 236. Eva Gothlin observes that while we do not have firm evidence for the precise Heidegger texts Beauvoir and Sartre read, by 1939, at least one text, Corbin's translation of "What is Philosophy" was widely available. See Eva Gothlin, "Reading Simone de Beauvoir with Martin Heidegger," in *The Cambridge Companion to Simone de Beauvoir*, 36.

a piece for an anthology he was editing, an essay that became the small book, *The Ethics of Ambiguity* in 1947.²⁵ Although her 1945 play, *Les Bouches Inutiles (Useless Mouths)* and her 1946 novel *Tous les hommes sont Mortels (All Men Are Mortal)* were not successful, criticized as clumsily disguised *roman à theses*, her 1949 phenomenological study of the status of women, *Les Deuxieme Sex (The Second Sex)* catapulted her into the stratosphere of major 20th century thinkers. Although its reception was polarized and in some cases antagonistic, this book changed her life in more ways than she may have liked, including her relationship to Sartre. After such a major undertaking, she nevertheless pursued ambitious literary projects, and won the Prix Goncourt for her comprehensive fictional treatment of the post-war intellectual struggle in France, 1954's *Les Mandarins*. Writing continuously during the 1950s and 60s, she produced a five volume autobiography, two travelogues, a collection of short stories, another major novel, and a study of old age. When asked whether she considered herself a philosopher, she replied, "I am a writer," which to her meant having the freedom to inscribe the problems and joys of the situated life in any form of literature.²⁶

Beauvoir's reputation as a gifted writer led to her very public engagement in political causes, along with Sartre. But these successes masked a troubling reality – that her "essential" relationship with Sartre had devolved into a professional liaison. The pain of his defection away from her decades of conversation, editorial service, and daily domestic organization towards younger and, to her mind, dangerous strangers adds another sad layer to the ambiguities of her life.²⁷ It is during this period that she radically changes her fictional focus, and publishes the novel *Les Belles Image*, and the collection of stories, *The Woman Destroyed*, both received

---

25  Beauvoir describes him as "a simple, cheerful soul" who "moved" her deeply with his response to *The Blood of Others*, "It's a fraternal book" (Beauvoir, *Prime of Life*, 444–45), a remark that satisfied Beauvoir's deepest ambition as a writer. However, later, in interviews with her biographer Deirdre Bair, she somewhat caustically complains about his condescension toward her early in their acquaintance. See Bair, *Simone de Beauvoir*, 290 f. 290–93.

26  Bair, *Simone de Beauvoir*, 269 cites here an interview with German feminist Alice Schwartzer, "After *The Second Sex*: Conversations with Simone de Beauvoir," 109.

27  Beauvoir herself, in *All Said and Done* and *A Farewell to Sartre*, defends the strength of their lifelong pact. However, her biographer Deirdre Bair shares Beauvoir's more honest and poignant appraisal of the pain of their later relationship, along with the acerbic observations of some of their close friends. This is more recently confirmed in Kate Kirkpatrick's intellectual biography, *Becoming Beauvoir: A Life* (London: Bloomsbury, 2019), 280.

somewhat ambivalently if not with downright hostility. Ironically, her self-perpetuating myth of unbreakable solidarity with Sartre also resulted in another misfortune, the mistaken belief that she was a mere parrot to Sartre's philosophical ideas, and not a major thinker in her own right.

The past 30 years of Beauvoir scholarship has laid this view to rest. A re-examination of her philosophical writings, along with the publication of her student journals and various correspondences leave no doubt that Simone de Beauvoir was a deeply read and gifted philosopher, one who may in fact have influenced Sartre.[28] The "riddle of influence" is not easily resolved, as both Beauvoir and Sartre came from similar backgrounds, resisting similar social and intellectual programs, and finding intellectual amitie with one another. However, influence aside, a waxing tide of scholarship re-examining Beauvoir's literature has established her acumen, subtlety and creativity within the European philosophical tradition. Pioneering scholars of Beauvoir's philosophy include Margaret Simons, Sara Heinämaa, Ursula Tidd and Deborah Berghoffen. They have inspired a legion of recent scholarship, in which Beauvoir's fluency with the tradition, especially the modern critical tradition inaugurated in Kant and Hegel, developed in Marx, Kierkegaard, Nietzsche, Freud, Bergson, Hussurl, and Heidegger, is met with her considerable powers of analysis.[29] In this operation in which she, like Derrida, contests what is unacceptable in the European tradition while affirming what gives it life, she shows herself as a true heir of the tradition, turning to face it honestly, critically, and with gratitude.

This re-investment in Beauvoir as philosopher is a welcome development. By contrast, Beauvoir is rarely viewed as a thinker of religion, and never from within a critical interrogation of religion. Those few studies that directly address Beauvoir and religion either try to argue she persists in operating according to a Catholic imagination, or that she displaces its codes with the tropes of existentialism. The category "religion," however,

---

28 See Christine Daigle and Jacques Colomb (eds) *Beauvoir and Sartre*.
29 See Debra Berghoffen, *The Philosophy of Simone de Beauvoir*; Penelope Deutscher's *The Philosophy of Simone de Beauvoir: Ambiguity, Conversion, Resistance* focuses her engagement with the "masters of suspicion;" Shannon M. Mussett and William S. Wilkerson (eds) *Beauvoir and Western Thought from Plato to Butler*. New York: SUNY Press, 2012. These studies exhibit the depth of Beauvoir's philosophical acumen, while arguing, in light of her creativity, for her continuing relevance in contemporary philosophy.

is assumed as self-evident,[30] against what I am arguing here. The common

[30] See Amy Hollywood, Eliane LeCarme Tabon and Joseph Mahon for the only specific discussion of Beauvoir and "religion." Mahon, in *Simone de Beauvoir and her Catholicism*, reviews the persistent vocabulary of French Roman Catholicism deployed throughout Beauvoir's texts, in the service of arguing that although she ceased to practice Catholicism, she continued to see the world through Catholic eyes, to the extent that her ethics are in fact an iteration of Roman Catholic ethics. However, the underlying purpose of his study is to establish and defend the ethics afforded by the Catholic imagination. Where one can sympathize with the notion that the formative forces of one's upbringing continue to resonate in one's maturity, Mahon is writing as an insider, with a confessional agenda, in which the interrogation of religion per se does not take place. Hollywood organizes her study, *Sensible Ecstasy: Mysticism, Sexual Difference, and the Demands of History*, around the curious attraction of four French atheist intellectuals to the mystic writers of the European tradition. In three sections, she reads the engagement with mystic writers in the works of George Bataille, Simone de Beauvoir, Jacques Lacan, and Luce Irigaray, situating the former within the discourse of the latter. One of the shorter chapters, "Mysticism is tempting," presents Beauvoir's approbation of Teresa of Avila in her own discussion of "The Mystic" in *The Second Sex*. In the course of presenting Beauvoir's discussion of Teresa, Hollywood also reads Beauvoir's own admission to "mystic" experiments, drawing a tangent between Beauvoir and Bataille in her claim that she "wanted to be everything." Hollywood presents Beauvoir's life and work as fraught with ambivalence, the avowed atheist existentialist who nevertheless remains attracted to an absolute. She claims that in Beauvoir's discussion of "religiosity," woman functions as man's other, and man, with "god," function for women in much the same way, an observation that is important to Beauvoir's philosophical response to alterity. While Hollywood seems to aim at a disruptive reading of the figure of female mystics as presented in Beauvoir, she seems most interested in arguing that "Beauvoir's early fascination with mysticism is tied to her uneasiness with limitation and mortality," a thesis with a much different scope than what I aiming for here. Eliane Lecarme-Tabone takes up the figure of "conversion" in her Introduction to Beauvoir's *Memoirs of a Dutiful Daughter*, in which she argues that Beauvoir subverts the term, moving away from "religion," toward the light of existentialism, at the same time that she exhibits precisely the characteristics of con-version, a turning with and through a new insight. She observes how Beauvoir repeats this re-appropriation of the tradition in her inversion of Pascal's wager: Pascal exhorts us to wager there is a god and to live accordingly, in order to keep our eligibility for the promised heaven; Beauvoir rejects this, wagering instead that the world is too beautiful to ignore now for a heaven that may not exist. Here we are introduced in a succinct way to a persistent movement in Beauvoir's thought – a dialectic of resistance and transformation that does not negate or sublate the original thesis but rather transforms it to new function.

understanding of the term "religion" has its place in this discussion, as those manifestations that are commonly called "religion" – those prescribed practices and beliefs – are performances of that play that is the "scene of religion." As I will argue in Chapter Two, the conditions of the French Bourgeoisie at the beginning of the 20th century expresses all of the forces involved in the reproduction of this scene, a scene of the dialectic between resistance and transformation.

Beauvoir's sensitivity to this dialectic may have its roots in that "endless disputation" between her parents as detailed in her memoir, as well as in the ambiguous circumstances of her youth. Above all, we must view Simone de Beauvoir in that moment of European history where she is subject to the force of bourgeois French society: the coalescing of church and capitalism into the social and political orthodoxy of the late 19th and early 20th century. This orthodoxy aims to reproduce itself through its mechanisms of gathering and binding – through its rigid codes of social conformity and Roman Catholic piety – mechanisms that at the same time produce forces of resistance – in literature, theatre, philosophy and apostasy. In this scene, as we will see when reviewing the memoir of Beauvoir's indoctrination and rebellion, the church is a ubiquitous social agency for the faithful, such as Françoise Brasseur, in which the appearance of piety and submission to the dogmatic prescriptions of the church ensure social as well as heavenly salvation. The capitalist drive to wealth acquisition, which establishes the formula: wealth= stability= social acceptability, acts as a counterpart to the hegemony of the church, with both inscribing a world of crushing demands for social, moral and financial purity. Inevitably, mechanically, such purity is contaminated by the same agents to which they appeal in a perpetual play of force and resistance.

Caught by the weight of these forces, Beauvoir, strikingly for her milieu, refuses conventional social norms of acquisition, domesticity and conjugal restraint. She seizes the moment to attain her education, and to become an intellectual when few women could conceive of such a life; she lived her "essential" yet "contingent" relationship with Sartre against the expectation of marriage and motherhood, loving openly Nelson Algren and Claude Lanzmann; at the same time, she was slow to become conscious of the ways in which "woman" has been subordinated and made other in most societies, and only obliquely acknowledged these forces in her own life. She lived thus in a situation of ambiguity and paradox, a movement of resistance within the scene of religion. This is also the scene of our other major characters, Jacques Derrida and Michel de Certeau.

There is no evidence of any direct concourse between Beauvoir, Certeau and Derrida. However, it is possible to locate biographical tangents. Derrida was deeply influenced by Sartre in his early education, and Certeau and Derrida knew and engaged with each other's discourse. These three literally walked the same streets of Paris in the early 1950s. Beauvoir had studied at the Sorbonne and haunted the district of *les écoles*, visiting her boyfriend Sartre and his circle of friends in the old Latin Quarter. Throughout her life, she continued to tread the ancient streets of the district to write in the cafe, Les Deux Magots. Like Sartre, Derrida was a *normalien*, studying for his *agrégation* at the École Normale Supérieure. The syllabus for philosophy students changed little in the 25 years between Beauvoir and Sartre's *agrégation* exams in 1929, and Derrida's successful second attempt in 1956. Certeau, educated at Grenoble, Lyon, and Les École des Hautes Études, (where Derrida taught for some time) eventually completed his Doctorate at the Sorbonne in 1960. Culturally and geographically, these three circulated in the same intellectual and social world, with many of the same interests and reservations, although for different reasons.

Derrida is perhaps the most infamous philosopher of the late 20th century, and possibly the most misunderstood, as he was received first by literary and cultural critics rather than philosophers. Derrida was born in 1930 to a Sephardic Jewish family in Algeria and came to philosophy, according to his own admission, through a "broadcast about Camus that set him on his path,"[31] likely around the same time that Camus was befriended by Sartre and Beauvoir. According to historian Edward Baring, in the late 1940s and early 1950s, in the French academic system, "for or against existentialism, nobody could ignore it."[32] In this milieu, Derrida read Sartre, and "from his earliest extant essays, those written when he was only 16 years old, Derrida showed an allegiance to existentialist philosophy, with an almost total reliance on Sartre's vocabulary,"[33] although at the same time, he "did not spare Sartre himself from criticism."[34] Existentialism was attractive to Derrida because it announced the possibility of a moral philosophy. Baring explicitly links Derrida to Beauvoir, in that they both seized on the opportunity to develop a moral philosophy:

---

31   Baring, *The Young Derrida*, 49. Baring cites the archived unpublished writings of Derrida when he was a philosophy student at the École Normale Supérieur in the early 1950s.
32   Baring, *The Young Derrida*, 50.
33   Baring, *The Young Derrida*, 50.
34   Baring, *The Young Derrida*, 50.

Derrida's emphasis on morality was not a lone response to Sartre's corpus. It was a focal point for numerous supporters and opponents, whether Francis Jeanson or Simone de Beauvoir's attempts at the construction of an atheistic existentialist morality or the Christian criticism of that very possibility.[35]

Derrida cites Sartre's "mantra" – "Man's existence precedes his essence" as a "path beyond moral nihilism."[36] For the student Derrida, "a will constrained to act in a particular way could not be regarded as moral,"[37] a phrase reminiscent of Beauvoir's assertion, that "moral consciousness can exist only to the extent that there is a disagreement between nature and morality. It would disappear if the ethical law became the natural law,"[38] since natural law by definition excludes choice and therefore the freedom it is founded upon. While Sartre's affirmation of absolute human freedom offered a philosophical basis for morality, one that could transcend nihilism, at the same time, Derrida saw Sartre as giving up on the possibility of outlining a moral system, and the possibility of transcendent value.[39] For this reason, although deeply marked by Sartre's account of the existential human condition, Derrida began to turn away from Sartre.

Like Beauvoir, in addressing humanism, Derrida tried to find an opening between the moral aporia of freedom and finitude: "The very acknowledgement of our insufficiency, our finitude, according to Derrida, marked the possibility of our surpassing it … With the possibility of transcendence, we could never recognize any particular measure as insufficient."[40] This is akin to Beauvoir's demand that philosophy embrace the ambiguities of our human condition. Baring says of Derrida's insight: "we are left caught between the dual immanence and transcendence of the measure; we are never certain of the legitimacy of any particular value, but in our constant desire to overcome our limitations, we continually reach for something better."[41] Similarly, for Beauvoir, human freedom justifies itself in the projects it undertakes, the shape and meaning of which are contingent and particular. She argues these "projects" constitute the only transcendence the existential consciousness can affirm: "The goal toward which I surpass myself must appear to me as a point of departure toward a new surpassing.

---

35 Baring, *The Young Derrida*, 50.
36 Baring, *The Young Derrida*, 51.
37 Baring, *The Young Derrida*, 51.
38 Beauvoir, *The Ethics of Ambiguity*, 10.
39 Baring, *The Young Derrida*, 52.
40 Baring, *The Young Derrida*, 79.
41 Baring, *The Young Derrida*, 80.

Thus, a creative freedom develops happily without ever congealing into unjustified facticity."[42]

In his student journal, Derrida referred to this period in his intellectual development as the period of *"existentiel spiritualism:"* Baring notes:

> The movement and progress of philosophy required both the recognition of our own limitations and the faint glimmer of an Absolute that would constantly incite us to cast off our earthly shackles and seek a deeper relationship with the divine. It was this tension between an immanence that could never full entrap us and transcendence that we could never fully achieve that constituted Derrida's "existentiel spiritualism."[43]

This label *"existentiel spiritualism"* might also describe the philosophy of Beauvoir, as she too acknowledges the tension between longing for an absolute transcendence one can never achieve and the finite fact of our situated mortality.[44] However, where Beauvoir adopts phenomenology as her method, Derrida, at the École Normale Supérieure, adopts Husserl's phenomenology as his object of study.[45] Despite refocusing his intellectual gaze, the problem of morality revealed in the existential consciousness, and an attendant attraction to "mysticism," continued to spur Derrida's investigations.

The point of departure between Beauvoir's intellectual touchstones and Derrida is also the point of contact and it involves Husserl. The "Problem of Genesis," the title of Derrida's École Normale Supérieure Mémoire begins with Husserl's last work, *The Origin of Geometry*." Through a discursive review of all of his texts, it concludes that Husserl can never resolve the aporia between the "world" as constituted, and the relationship to the subject as "constituting." This unresolvable problem in Husserl captures Derrida's attention, to the extent that his *avant-propos* to his project is entitled "History of Philosophy and Philosophy of History,"[46] wherein he explains that his aim "was to show how philosophy both was anchored in its time and transcended it, was both constituted and constituting."[47] While Derrida began his Mémoire as "a classic Normalien project, a study of the conditions of the possibility for scientific objectivity,"[48] his turn to

---

42 Beauvoir, *The Ethics of Ambiguity*, 27.
43 Baring, *The Young Derrida*, 80.
44 Beauvoir, *The Ethics of Ambiguity*, 5.
45 Baring, *The Young Derrida*, 82.
46 Baring, *The Young Derrida*, 142.
47 Baring, *The Young Derrida*, 143.
48 Baring, *The Young Derrida*, 144.

Husserl provided him with "a vehicle for discussing older themes," especially "mysticism." Derrida begins by investigating the connection between scientific objectivity and psychology, and through his engagement with Husserl, makes his central problematic "the articulation of truth and time, science and history. Or in French: *épistémologie*."[49]

The phenomenological affinity between Derrida and Beauvoir shows Beauvoir enthusiastically seizing on Husserlian phenomenology as method,[50] although open to its reformulations in Merleau-Ponty.[51] Derrida is more interested in its central problematic, the epistemological aporia of the relationship between the perceiver and the perceived, whether the phenomena is constituted or constituting. He soon turns to other resources for articulating this aporia and its attendant consequences. This is clearly the first of an elliptical cycle of figures in Derrida's thought that is ultimately construed as the logic of *différance*, the non-negotiable play of differences that, in perpetual tension, destabilizes the concept of identity, of "presence," of the possibility of ontology classically conceived. The problem of the constituted and the constituting in Husserl, seized upon by Derrida, can also be described as a figure of "ambiguity." But where Beauvoir, the philosopher of existential ethics, exhorts us to embrace ambiguity as an axiom for acting responsibly, Derrida, the philosopher of epistemology, interrogates ambiguity – its figures, its mechanisms, and its limits. His interrogations offer a structure of performance within which to understand Beauvoir's displacement of "religion" as she composes her existential ethic.

Derrida's earliest writings show that he affirmed an existential perspective. Not given to labelling himself, he nevertheless persists in interrogating the axiom of individual *responsibility*, an unavoidable figure of European thought that he will examine in *The Gift of Death,* "Passions: An Oblique Offering," *Spectres of Marx*, and "Force of Law," among others. Like Beauvoir, Derrida persistently returns to the figures of religion, mysticism, and faith as objects of inquiry throughout his career because they constitute the inheritance to which he responds. Like Beauvoir, Derrida suspected institutional religion, but did not tire of interrogating it.

If Sartre and existentialism provide a common focus between Beauvoir and Derrida, then Hegel and the mystics join Beauvoir and Derrida with

---

49 Baring, *The Young Derrida*, 145.
50 Beauvoir recounts her enthusiasm for Husserlian phenomenology in *The Prime of Life*, 162.
51 Beauvoir gave an informed and sympathetic review of Merleau-Ponty's *The Phenomenology of Perception* for *Les Temps Moderne* in 1945.

Certeau.[52] Certeau's magnum opus, *The Mystic Fable*, and his previous study of Jean Joseph Surin, inquisitor at Loudun, in *The Possession at Loudun*, consumed much of his academic career. Born to a privileged family in 1925, Certeau studied philosophy and classics at Grenoble and Lyon before joining the Jesuit order in 1956. Like Beauvoir and Derrida, Certeau developed a deep attraction to psychoanalytic theory, even becoming a founding member of Lacan's École Freudienne, despite never undergoing a psychoanalysis. In 1960, he earned his doctorate from the Sorbonne for the study of religious history. Like Beauvoir, Certeau devoted himself to reading Hegel and, according to his literary executor, Luce Giard, having joined "the special one-year program dedicated to Hegel's philosophy: the 'happy few' spent one full year, for six hours every day, in close reading and commenting of Hegel, read in the German text."[53] This echoes Beauvoir's observation, "why reading the Hegelian system is so comforting. I remember having experienced a great feeling of calm on reading Hegel in the impersonal framework of the *Bibliothèque Nationale* in August 1940."[54] Beauvoir, Certeau and Derrida each reflect deeply upon the Hegelian account of the self and the other, a figure that drives each of their projects. Marian Füssell observes that:

> The dialectics between ego and other, identity and alterity clearly show the influence of Hegel and Lacan on Certeau. Like many other French Jesuits of his time, he was affected by Joseph Gauvins' reading of Hegel and he was a member of Lacan's École Freudienne for many years. I is other .... The 'problem of history' is for Certeau 'inscribed in the place of this subject, which is itself a play of difference, the historicity of a nonidentity with itself,'[55]

a sentiment that just as easily describes the concerns of Beauvoir and Derrida.

---

52  Derrida's essay "*Sauf le Nom*" is a reading of Angelus Silesius' *The Cherubinic Wanderer* in *On the Name*. Beauvoir attests to her long engagement with the 16th and 17th century mystical texts in *Memoirs of a Dutiful Daughter*, including Angelus Silesias, as well as devoting a chapter to the "mystics" in *The Second Sex*, which I will examine in Chapter Four.

53  Giard, "Michel de Certeau's Biography: Petite Bibliographie en anglais." Jesuites.com, February 5, 2006, http://www.jesuites.com/histoire/certeau.htm#bio. Website 12 March 2017.

54  Beauvoir, *The Ethics of Ambiguity*, 158.

55  Füssel, "Writing the Otherness – The Historiography of Michel de Certeau SJ," in Bocken, *Spiritual Spaces: History and Mysticism in Michel de Certeau*, edited by Inigo Bocken (Leuven, Peeters Publishing, 2013), 31.

A member of the Jesuit community until his death, Certeau exhibits a sympathy and dexterity with what might be called an existential perspective in his writing. William Friijhoff claims:

> Certeau's faith was for him a kind of 'existential imperative' on both fronts: as a believer and, as some have characterized him, as a mystic. He stood at a far remove from the rationalism of the God-deniers – for Certeau a chimerical struggle without an object – but also from the Christianity of emotions, from the sacral claims of the established churches, and from their legalistic, politicized, or moralistic behavior.[56]

Recognized as a brilliant polymath, in his critical stance toward historiography, in his insistence on situating the object of inquiry despite its limits, in his sensitivity to the embodied experience of living:

> Certeau lived his life and shaped his scholarship out of everyday experience, the conviction that life, and therefore history as well, is essentially a practice, an *acte de faire* realized in the act of appropriation by the subject. His definition of culture was therefore an active one ...[57]

Such an active definition of culture resonates with Derrida's figure of deconstruction, that different logic that is always unfolding, instantiating, contaminating, deferring, and differing. Certeau's investigations as a historian of "heterology," indebted to the Hegelian dialectic, to Lacanian psychoanalysis, to deconstruction and a certain historiography comman culminate in *The Mystic Fable*.

Beauvoir regularly speaks of "religion," although she does not interrogate the term "religion" in any explicit way in her autobiographical account of growing up in a French Roman Catholic bourgeois milieu. She simply assumes of her reader a familiarity with that tradition – its teachings, practices, expectations – as well as an implicit understanding that it belongs to the self-evident category, "religion," and then witnesses her own responses to it. However, in *The Second Sex, All Said and Done* and *The Coming of Age*, she writes about "religion" as an object of examination with scholarly sophistication, although she does not document her sources except in a most general way. In *The Second Sex*, Beauvoir gives a psychological and sociological analysis of "mysticism" based on her own readings of the mystic tradition of the 14th to 17th centuries, one that anticipates

---

56 Willima Frijhoff, "Michel de Certeau (1925–1986) – A Multifaceted Intellectual," in Bocken, *Spiritual Spaces: History and Mysticism in Michel de Certeau*, 17.
57 Frijhoff, "Michel de Certeau" (1925–1986), 18.

Amy Hollywood's schematic approach to mysticism in her study, *Sensible Ecstasy*.[58] In *All Said and Done,* she explicitly addresses the issue of her own atheism, with regard to those who lamented she had not had a proper exposure to "real Christians" or "an intelligent priest."[59] She assures us that she can quote Gospel passages by heart and that her "religious instruction was in fact very thorough."[60] In *The Coming of Age,* her review of the subject of old age in the "ethnological" and historical records refers to what, at that time, the late 1970s, was state of the art scholarship on ancient Near Eastern myth as well as critical biblical scholarship. She is thoroughly acquainted with critical exegesis, and with its interdisciplinary reliance on archeological, historical, textual, formal and source criticism. Because of this critical stance, she shows no sympathy towards the essentialist, universalist metaphysics of those who take a *sui generis* approach to religion. She does, however, acknowledge a certain indebtedness to the "ethnologists," and in particular her friend and colleague Claude Levi-Strauss.[61] This acknowledgement suggests both her structuralist and sociological approach to much of this "data," as she views these traditions and their narratives as iterations of the uncritically received "serious" worldview that her philosophy consistently rejects.

It is important to acknowledge as we proceed that "religion" is examined in relation to Beauvoir in two registers. When presenting Beauvoir's biographical account of her pious childhood and eventual rejection of French Roman Catholicism, "religion" is presented according to Beauvoir's own uninterrogated usage, sophisticated though it is, a usage related to but not to be confused with the critical treatment of religion I propose. Before undertaking an in-depth review of Beauvoir's reflections on her culturally received experience of Roman Catholicism and her rejection of that institution's practices and beliefs, I will describe the critical performative structure needed for understanding both her milieu and her philosophy – the scene of religion.

---

58 Hollywood's study aims, in part, to interrogate the relationship between gender and "mystic" mode in Sensible Ecstasy: Mysticism, Sexual Difference, and the Demands of History (Chicago: University of Chicago Press, 2002), testing the claims of a corollary between woman with erotic/embodied "mysticism," versus man with cerebral/spiritual "mysticism," enlisting psychological, sociological and political criticism.
59 Beauvoir, *All Said and Done,* 459.
60 Beauvoir, *All Said and Done,* 459.
61 Beauvoir, *The Coming of Age,* 44–45.

## Chapter 2
# Setting the Scene

### I. AT THE MARGINS OF RELIGION

To argue that the atheist existentialist Beauvoir is a thinker of religion requires an account of the category "religion." A review of the academic interrogation of religion will situate the view of religion I am proposing here – the scene of religion revealed in the writing of Jacques Derrida. We stand at the margins of religion in a number of senses. Derrida reads religion as the all encompassing scene that so penetrates our world it can only be seen at all from the margins. He also proposes the figure of margin, marginality, as a sign of undecideability: thinking at the margins requires thinking things that are not clearly one or the other, that are, to use Beauvoir's language, ambiguous. In another register, Beauvoir, Derrida and Certeau also understand themselves to be "marginal," in the sense of resisting the mainstream of the traditions that we commonly call religion in their own lives. Thus, this study proposes a working theory of religion as a ubiquitous structure only detectable at the margins, articulated by thinkers who understand themselves as intellectually marginal.

In its common sense, religion signals a set of beliefs and practices, usually underwritten by metaphysical claims, prescribed by an authoritative institution. Alternatively, it can refer to an ineffable, transient but powerful feeling that seems to convey a kind of knowledge. We usually name this experience "spirituality," but still categorize it as a kind of religion. However, these common notions of religion, familiar and obvious though they may seem, do not convey the problem with the category religion which has occupied academics for the past 30 years.

In the early 21st century, the interrogation of "religion" by critical theorists of religion reveal it as an amorphous and ill-defined category of human activity, largely governed and disseminated by European colonial forces, with small regard for the accuracy or appropriateness of its use. Minimally, they argue that religion is a construction that serves the scholar's interests; more dramatically, it is presented as a ubiquitous machinery that advances the forces of global capitalism and the tele-technocracy that supports it. In the past 30 years, the discipline of Religious Studies has undergone a theoretical revolution.[1] Thirty years ago, nascent departments of Religious Studies, particularly in North American universities, struggled to establish a disciplinary identity, distinct from Faculties of Theology. Early on, departments sought to demonstrate the "science" in the study of religion-as-object, through multi-disciplinary approaches: anthropology, archeology, psychology, philosophy, sociology and literary criticism. However, the implicit and uncritically held theory informing these approaches, variously called the *sui generis* or essentialist account of religion, was not broadly questioned. The structuralist essentialism of Mircea Eliade, editor of the *Encyclopedia of Religion*, served as the dominant paradigm for scholars of religion: that is, the view that all "religions" witness a universal truth, inflected in distinct traditions. This paradigm was an ideal choice for a relatively new discipline that needed to clearly distinguish itself from the confessional strictures of traditional theology, while not posing a threat to that universal metaphysical truth to which the essentialist position claims all religious traditions respond.

The continental philosophical discourse of the 1960s and 1970s, including Derrida, continued the tradition of Critical Theory, interrogating the intellectual, political and social assumptions of the European Enlightenment. The debates that this entailed led to the emergence of new theoretical paradigms for the study of religion in the late 1980s and early

---

1 It must be noted that the study of religion as an object of inquiry has a much longer tradition, perhaps beginning with Humbolt and Schliermacher in the late 18th and early 19th centuries and their fascination with the texts of India and the ancient Near East, respectively. The currents of European philosophical thought in the 19th century, two world wars, and the intellectual response to this, profoundly influenced the study of religion there, and the "discipline" in Europe has had a different trajectory. See Kippenberg, *Discovering Religious History in the Modern Age* for this history. There is no doubt that the study of religion in North America echoes developments in Europe, but slowly, and in a very different context. See McCutcheon, *Manufacturing Religion* for a review and critique of the North American version of discipline.

1990s. A new generation of scholars for the first time examined the classification "religion."

J.Z. Smith famously declared, "there is no data for religion,"[2] not only no way of verifying or measuring the essentialist, metaphysical claims of the many traditions called "religion," but also no way of escaping the constructed character of the very categories we name to determine the genus. Smith's insight opened the way for a range of interrogations of religion, leading some scholars to conclude that religion is simply a species of human behavior, one that is not categorically different from other human behaviors. Those who accept this proposition are faced with the decision to either study human traditions labelled "religion" as anthropological, psychological or sociological data, or else, as Anne Taves[3] has argued, to study it through ascription, that is, as data that the practitioner "deems to be religious." Such an approach offers the scholar a way to reflect on the popular notion of religion – that it names the response to an essential and or universal truth that gives meaning and guidance to life.

Another fertile paradigm has been the interrogation of religion as a situated constructed category within the power structures of a given scene. For example, Russell McCutcheon argues that in the United States, religion is a category manufactured by the powerful as a tool for hegemony, domestically and internally.[4] In a similar vein, Timothy Fitzgerald argues that the category "religion" is no longer viable at all, merely masking what is effectively a vague liberal theology that derails serious socio-political cultural analysis.[5] On a broader scale, Tomoko Masuzawa examines the genealogy of the world religions paradigm, showing that it appears as a category only as post-enlightenment European scholars discover a civilization older and more complex than Christendom in the Vedas and Pali sutras. In response to this potential displacement of European superiority, they invent the category "world religions" in a way that reinforces the biases of their "Orientalism," while asserting Europe as the natural heir and presumptive improvement on India. Masuzawa argues that, while putatively affirming a "universal essence" to which all religions respond, the category of world religions functions to perpetuate the stereotypes of Eurocentricity and its

---

2 Smith, *Imagining Religion*, 3.
3 See Taves, *Religious Experience Reconsidered* in which her main argument is for ascription as a way out of the impasse presented by accepting the limits of coherent discourse on the metaphysical claims of traditions.
4 See McCutcheon, *Manufacturing Religion*.
5 See Fitzgerald, *The Ideology of Religion*.

impoverished understanding of the other.[6] Hans Kippenberg reviews much of the same documentary evidence as Masuzawa, but takes a more sympathetic tactic, calling the "discovery" of world religions a construct that helped post-enlightenment believers and skeptics to clarify their understanding of their own tradition and their own theoretical commitments in relation to it.[7] For Kippenberg, the very emergence of a discourse of world religions is the European intellectuals' response to modernity. As he notes, prior to the Enlightenment, no one would use the term "religion" to identify ones' traditions and practices. Rather, until very recently, one spoke of "nations" rather than "religion," and then only in the European context.

At present, there is no broad consensus about what it means to study religion, nor even what the word signifies. Many critically informed scholars continue to offer the World Religion Paradigm in their introductory courses, even while acknowledging its fraught political and theoretical history. Those who are committed to theoretical consistency may still endorse the essentialist view of religion, while others who reject this view will persist in examining those things "deemed religious," without theorizing why this category, "things deemed religious," require a distinct discipline. Some of the scholars cited here reject the entire idea of the discipline as a discrete field of inquiry, and argue the work of scholars of religion can just as effectively be carried out in other disciplines, such as psychology, sociology, history and cultural studies.

Many of these perspectives inform Derrida's reading of religion, but he brings to the discussion a different framework, the logic of *différance*. As a philosopher of this different logic, one pursued through a performative regime of reading deconstructively, Derrida examines the machinery of replication and reproduction in European civilization, unveiling the possibility of disruption, of *l'avenir*, in a perpetual play of undecideability.

Somewhat inexplicably, Derrida is not read widely among critical theorists of religion, although he is much embraced by cultural theorists, literary critics and continental philosophers. The same is true of Michel de Certeau, whose monumental *The Mystic Fable* receives less notice than his study of cultural heterology, *The Practice of Everyday Life*. Like Derrida, Certeau inhabits the margins of the academic study of religion, and is far more likely to be debated within cultural studies, literary criticism, and amongst theologians.[8]

---

6 Masuzawa, *The Invention of World Religions*.
7 Kippenberg, *Discovering Religious History in the Modern Age*, 34.
8 The academic study of religion is radically distinct from theology in that it treats its object, "religion," as an object subject to critical assessment. Theology

This raises the question, why read Beauvoir against these two thinkers, both of whom inhabit the margins of critical discourse in the study of religion? First, because Derrida's interrogation of religion amounts to both a philosophical investigation of its genealogy and a critique of European metaphysics. He proposes that the "self" that we inherit, the self that is at play in the self-other dialectic and whose "rights" are underwritten by Enlightenment ideals, is inaugurated in the Holy Roman Empire and develops with it and its offspring. This self attains its distinctive self-consciousness in response to the appeal of the one, the one who demands we make holy its truths. This has a crucial bearing on Beauvoir's ethic, which is an existential response to the self-other dialectic, in which the situated singular self makes meaning in response to an other situated singularity. Second, this conception of self that Beauvoir inherits is given a more granular historical genealogy in Certeau. His study of the mystics is as much a study of a certain play in the psychology of the self, a self who is in mourning. This iteration of the self-conscious self mourns for that One who is absent: that one who is neither the Church, nor hidden in scripture, nor found in the experience of bodily communion, nor in the empty tomb. It is a mourning for no-thing, which launches the perpetual wanderings of those who continue to search, a path doomed to be a *via negativa*. The scene of religion emerging from the late Rennaissance mystics eventually arrives at the denial of that "knowledge" that demands indemnification, and the arising of the existential stance. Situating Beauvoir's philosophy of ambiguity within the play of this scene offers a new and more urgent significance to her ethical injunctions.

The scene of religion presented here, while founded in the texts of Derrida, neither aspires nor pretends to be a definitive statement of Derrida's "theory of religion." Derrida's many readings of texts that bear on the question of religion will keep us occupied for a long time to come. However, the thread that I am pulling here has merit for understanding the significance of Beauvoir's ethic against Derrida's critical insights. Certeau, as an heir to the same tradition and as an ally of deconstruction, provides a situated historical play of the scene in question, one which clairifes the "I-Other" play and the faith it requires that is at the heart of Beauvoir's ethic.

---

by its nature is concerned with the explication and defense of dogma, rather than the interrogation of it. Theology should never be confused for the critical study of religion, even acknowledging that there can be relevant overlaps between the two disciplines.

## II. "RELIGION" AND THE "SELF:" A GENEALOGY

The thread I wish to follow in Derrida is primarily drawn from "Faith and Knowledge," and *The Gift of Death*. In these texts, Derrida considers the genealogy of "responsibility" and draws a direct line from the Greco-Judeo-Christian theology of the first century to the 20th century figure of capitalist economy. The philosopher of *différance* reads the European figure of religion according to this different logic, tracing the mechanisms of reproduction and iteration – those forces that compose and dismantle – within the scene of religion. Derrida thinks with his readers by reading specific texts in order to expose the mechanism of deconstruction within them. Some preliminary acknowledgement of the scope of the "different logic" seen in Derrida's deconstructions of texts, deconstructions grounded in his thorough familiarity with the philosophical tradition, is required.

Every figure in Derrida's lexicon is an iteration of *différance*, the non-negotiable logic of every "N" promising a "+1," an *alternative*, an other possibility, that exists whether taken or not, an alternative that is always a threat as well as an affirmation.[9] *Différance* suggests both to differ – as in to be different, to be other than, as such, as well as to defer – to delay carrying the import, meaning, or consequence of the thing in question, to reserve. Such consequences inhabit a blind spot that the performance of deconstruction upturns. It is crucial to observe that *différance* is conceived as something written, that the "a" in its spelling cannot be perceived by the ear when pronounced. The odd spelling is only accessible in its written/read form. In a move that alludes to *Of Grammatology*, and the argument there in which speech and the chain of privilege afforded to it – presence, being, and, ultimately, static eternal metaphysics – is contested, the emphasis here on this distinction which is only detectable in writing is a performance of this very logic. This logic demonstrates that presence, being, "is-ness" (and its entire chain of meanings) are not stable; that all things are, like writing, already coursing another path, separate from the moment of the undertaking, already deferred, for another, later reader and reading. Peggy Kamuf quotes Derrida's economical, idiomatic and therefore untranslatable expression of this in "Plato's Pharmacy," where:

> Locating this different logic in writing is of course also a performance of the assertion that we might turn our attention toward writing as a more adequate figure for understanding our world. It is movement, both spatial

---

9 See Jacques Derrida's "Différance" in *Margins of Philosophy* for this specific account of the logic of différance.

and temporal: the production of differences, of that which differentiates and of delay, deferral, and detouring. Textuality being constituted by differences and by differences from differences, it is by nature absolutely heterogeneous and is constantly *composing with* [emphasis added] the forces that tend to annihilate it. (98)[10]

This figure of *writing*, as a "composing with the forces that tend to annihilate it" is, as Kamuf notes, an untranslatable but succinct performance of the machinery of this logic. It is the figure that perhaps offers an accessible structure for understanding the manifold other figures in Derrida's prolific body of work, such as *khora*, the *pharmakon*, autoimmunity, spectrality, mourning, inheritance, messianicity, to begin a list too long to continue.[11]

In the texts we will follow here, the "other" figures in many iterations: both as singular persons located in the world, and as a signifier for "all others," for the space of "otherness," or as Derrida puts it, "*tout autre est tout autre*."[12] Derrida sees in this dialectic a play of *différance*. On the one hand, there is the desire to sublate the other, to make the other the same, to gather and bind that which is other into a homogeneity, a totality; on the other hand, this gathering and binding is undone by the logic of *différance*: that is, the desiring self can only find fulfillment in destroying an other self-consciousness; and yet, the self becomes aware of her dependence on that other self-consciousness and by inference, its otherness. It is aware of the other's awareness of the self: it experiences *recognition*. Thus, the desire to sublate or unify is undone in its own movement. Following this logic in Hegel's dialectic, the logic of the inherent requirement of recognition for the self and the other, one must recognize the other in order to define the self. This heterogeneous movement at play undermines the drive to homogeneity, as well as opening onto the future, to possibilities, to "messianicity without messianism."[13] This brief expliqué of the play of *différance* Derrida reads in the Hegelian dialectic of self is also a warning: Derrida

10 Quoted in Kamuf, "Composition Displacement," 878.
11 See McCance, *Sleights of Hand*; and Naas, *Miracle and Machine* for a thorough yet succinct presentation of these and other figures in Derrida.
12 Derrida, *The Gift of Death and Literature in Secret*, 69.
13 Derrida, "Faith and Knowledge," 83 f. 83–84. Derrida again suggests a structuring play at work that exceeds all determinate situations: here, the movement of "messianicity" which exceeds all instances of "messianism," suggesting that this movement is an openness to the possibility of an opening out of oppression, hegemony, totalizing, binding and gathering forces, an openness he also calls "*l'avenir*," which at the same time includes the "possibility of radical evil, without which the good would be for nothing" (Derrida, "Faith and

does not offer arguments per se, nor conventional theories, although he does follow a rigorous path of inquiry. The only way to follow his deconstructions, always located in specific texts, is to follow his deconstructions, wherein the mechanisms of composition and anhiliation perform.

In his densest engagement with the question of religion, "Faith and Knowledge: The Two Sources of Religion at the Limit of Reason Alone," Derrida inherits the tradition of Europe by turning to interrogate it. His starting point is the European Enlightenment, and the response to the "death of God" revealed by the 18th century philosophers of Reason, Kant and Hegel. In responding to their critiques, Derrida reads on the one hand, their inability to escape the metaphysics of the Christian religious tradition they re-vision; and on the other hand, how religion and the axiomatic "self" assumed in their philosophies may provide the conditions for a universalizable justice to come.

The scene of religion that I read in Derrida is that structure of play between, on the one hand, that knowledge which demands to be made holy and which requires indeminification, historically called God, the Good, the Truth etc., and on the other hand, the faith that is offered by the self in response to the appeal of this authority. Derrida suspects the former – the idea of knowledge that demands indemnification – because the logic of *différance* undermines such absolutes. He privileges the latter – faith – because it is an act that exceeds the precincts of religiosity, an act that procedes from what he names an "invincible hope for justice." This faith also proceeds from that inexhaustible space beyond space, that unthinkable place of the originary, beyond reason and time, indicated by the Platonic figure of *Khora*. It is faith that permits and gives meaning to that originary promise to believe each other, even at the risk of betrayal, and it is thus the foundation for all of our relationships. Perhaps, he suggests, these relationships are the true locus for any "salvation," through the openess afforded for the justice of that which is to come, a belief I argue is consistent with Beauvoir's ethic. Above all, he reads religion as "the response," the promise to believe the one who appeals to us, the other who has promised us the truth. This exchange of promises between self and other, which requires response – pledging, swearing, promising again – holds in its custody the hope for justice to come, a justice that we heirs of the Enlightenment might look for in a "universalizable culture of

---

Knowledge," 83). This openness is itself built into the play of *différance*, here presented in the figure of autoimmunity.

singularities," Derrida's precise summary of what is worth inheriting from the Enlightenment.

The essay, "Faith and Knowledge," originated at a conference in Capri in 1994, in which a popular claim of the 1990s, that the world was seeing a "return to the religious" was interrogated. This "return" was marked by the evidence of various violences performed in the name of religion, as well as the emerging political influence of certain Christian sects in the United States. A telling feature of this essay is that it is presented in two fonts, each assigned to one half of the essay. The first section is labelled "*ITALICS*," in italic font; the second section is labelled "POST SCRIPTUM," in Roman font. This seems to suggest a perspective from the margins that we, the readers, can partake in: that which is printed in the italic font perhaps allows us to see that which is printed in the Roman font differently, just as the site of the conference that inaugurated this discourse, Capri, might give its discussants a perspective from the margins on "Rome." In acknowledging this distinction, we may intellectually give ourselves a *theoria* by which to view the ubiquitous heritage of Rome at play in our contemporary context.

Derrida begins by drawing a philosophical line between the Greco-Roman light of Platonic knowledge, and Immanuel Kant. He evokes, on the one hand, Kant's argument for the reasonability of theistic belief and, on the other hand, his injunction that to will morally, we must do so as though God were absent. In this, Kant serves as a bridge between the pre-capitalist Latin imperial-ecclesiastical world and the present global-capitalist imperialism pulsating, above all, from the United States. He also invokes the play of the "self" and "other" in its Greco-Roman European iteration, and reads the emergence of this self accompanying the development of Roman Christianity and its "religion."

Derrida asserts that "religion" is clearly embedded in the globalatinization, his coinage for the empire of technological-capitalism that is the dominant paradigm of our globe. The complexity of this interpenetration of society, politics and ecnoemy belies any simple claim of a return to religion. He suggests that "religion" is inescapable for the contemporary world, much as the ocean is to the fish who swim in it. He draws this interpretation out of a consideration of three specific philosophical texts: Kant's *Religion Within the Limits of Reason Alone*, in which Kant asserts two forms of religion, the performative or "cultic" and the "reflective," the latter of which Kant argues is the only moral religion; Hegel's *Faith and Knowledge*, in which Hegel makes the case for the union of reason and spirit, according to his dialectic of history; and Bergson's "Two Sources of Morality and

Religion," in which he argues for the dual nature of the human, animal and creator, devising two kinds of societies, open and closed.[14] Without limiting himself to a specific Heidegger text, Derrida also takes on the figure of ontotheology, which Derrida argues is contaminated by a residue of presence that undoes its intention. All of these texts are alluded to in the full title of the essay. "Faith and Knowldege: The Two Sources of Religion at the Limit of Reason Alone."

Derrida argues for the distinctly European origin of "relgion" through the etymology of the word: "*European, it was first of all Latin ... Difficult to say 'Europe' without connoting: Athens-Jerusalem-Rome-Byzantium, wars of religion,*"[15] In typical fashion, we are plunged into a space of indetermination, where the boundaries are porous, exceeding those named. The European is itself the result of polyvalent Mediterranean and Middle Eastern traditions, and this immediately forces a recognition, that in this discussion the absolute and the definitive as categories will bleed away, into other margins. It is within this ambiguous space and history that he locates the mechanism of religion, one informed by that "knowledge" which Plato and Christianity configured as "light." Weaving a chain between figures of "light," "enlightenment," and "illumination," he connects these to the Sanskrit root, "*deivos*," – which denotes "luminous," and "celestial."[16] All of these figures of illumination lead to the Kantian theme of "reflection," and Derrida's insistence "on the relation of all religion to fire and to light. There is the light of revelation and the light of the Enlightenment:[17] both require a response, offering a knowledge that needs to be made "safe and sound," "holy," and "unscathed."

---

14 See Alexandre Lefebvre and Melanie White, "Introduction" in Lefebvre and White, *Bergson, Politics and Religion*, 10 in which they cite his famous closing lines: "In sum, we are simultaneously animal and creator, a point captured in the remarkable closing lines of Two Sources: 'Mankind lies groaning, half crushed beneath the weight of its own progress. Men do not sufficiently realize that their future is in their own hands. Theirs is the task of determining first of all whether they want to go on living or not. Theirs the responsibility, then, for deciding if they want merely to live, or intend to make just the extra effort required for fulfilling, even on their refractory planet, the essential function of the universe, which is a machine for the making of gods' (ts317/1245). This incarnation of the theological in the political, and their essential entanglement, is a theme taken up repeatedly."
15 Derrida, "Faith and Knowledge," 44.
16 Derrida, "Faith and Knowledge," 46.
17 Derrida, "Faith and Knowledge," 77.

He observes that Kant's definition of "reflecting faith," a faith identified with Christianity, requires that in order to act morally in accordance with the categorical imperative, one must act as though God does not exist.[18] The inference here is that the source of knowledge, the "God" to whom one responds in faith, swearing to believe, becomes absent in the light of Kant's categorical imperative, dependent as it is only upon a good will and a capacity to reason. However, replacing the authority of God with the reason that enables the good will of the moral person instatiates reason as a cipher for that same authority. The authority of that Being who is identical to the eternal and absolute truth is replaced by that which is logically, universally "true," a substitute truth, which the Enlightenment forces of gathering and binding indemnify. This is a moment in which the style of authority is relayed and reassigned, from the tradition of absolute deity to the supremacy of autonomous reason. This establishes the conditions for one of Derrida's theses here, that there is no opposition between faith and knowledge, between religion and reason, because both are implicated in the same play between, on the one hand, indemnifying certain truths and, on the other hand, promising to believe those truths even if they might be perjuries or lies. The authority of God, whom we traditionally call upon to witness our faithfulness, our willingness to believe and indemnify, is now replaced by the Light of Reason, reason which functions in the same way, attesting to the universalizable truth of our moral judgement.

Derrida observes the absence of the One to whose absolute presence we may promise our belief, implying his existential stance regarding traditional metaphysics. Today, instead of pledging to the truth offered by the One, we have instead the prescriptions of globalatinized capitalism, which are nevertheless founded in a tradition of an absolute authority, an authority in which the absent One haunts the "present:" "Everything begins with the presence of *that absence*"[19] – which is to say, that the God of the Abrahamic traditions, the God whom Christianity claims has died, is nevertheless "present" in the definitive sense, as an eternal absolute intelligible truth that the responders pledge to believe, identical to the eternal sunshine of Plato's intelligible realm.[20] This other person, this God, this inaccessible other, "Being itself," is conversely identical to the "presence"

---

18  Derrida, "Faith and Knowledge," 49.
19  Derrida, "Faith and Knowledge," 65.
20  See Derrida, *The Gift of Death*, 5, in which he considers Jan Patocka's contention that Christianity retains both the Platonic Form of the Good and the pre-Platonic "orgiastic," the "demonic" in which no responsibility is possible.

upon which all knowledge, in the Platonic and subsequently European sense, depends.

From this analysis, he observes that Christianity has always announced the death of god, and so has arrived at a contemporary state of "madness," of a globalatinzed capitalist world that is still "speaking Latin,"[21] and is "running out of breath,"[22] as it demands the indemnification of law by means of a force that undermines its intent. It speaks Latin to the extent that the paradigm of Latin (Greco-Roman) metaphysical assumptions still circulate in our discourse, the discourse of "being" generated in the use of "is," "presence," "world," "proper," "rights," "law," and all those things founded in the assertions of metaphysical truth inherited in the Roman. It is "madness" to the extent that "*Religion* circulates in the world one might say like an English word (*comme un mot anglais*) that has been to Rome and taken a detour to the United States."[23] In its name is spread and imposed through global capitalism an imperial political-military hegemony, a violent hegemony, that still calls on the absent god to be its witness, a witness to things "which have always been and remain foreign to what this word names and arrests in its history."[24]

Further querying the etymology of the term religion, a term his fellow discussants seem to use in a confident and self-evident way, he locates it first in its two possible Latin roots, *religere* and *religare*, one denoting "to gather," the other denoting "to bind."[25] The question is, what is it that is gathered and bound? The answers are multiple, but as with any formulation of "essence," "presence," and "sovereignity," to gather and to bind is to attempt to make things "move no more," to enforce a comforting and illusory stasis upon a thing that will always exceed, according to the logic of *différance*, such attempts at containment. The impulse to gather and to

---

21 Derrida, "Faith and Knowledge," 5.
22 Derrida, "Faith and Knowledge," 67.
23 Derrida, "Faith and Knowledge," 67.
24 Derrida, "Faith and Knowledge," 65. This is one of many oblique references to violence – to contemporary "wars of religion," those conflicts of the late 20th century arising out of conflicting religious identities, for example, Northern Ireland, Iraq, India etc., including the 1982 massacre at Chatila, as well as those other violences – industrial slaughter in food production, the fatwa against Salman Rushdie, the violent oppression of women in "Islamicist" states, etc. Derrida refers to Genet, who witnessed the massacre at Chatila (the 1993 interview, *Genet à Chatila*), which he states offers several of the themes under consideration in "Faith and Knowledge," especially "the question of religion."
25 Derrida, "Faith and Knowledge," 71.

bind will construct the phantasm[26] of those indeminified and yet debatable truths that haunt our world, here in the binaries of father/son, high/low, eternal/temporal, heavenly/worldly, spirit/body, male/female, sinner/saint, etc. Above all, it is to attempt to fix the thing, to make it reproducible, to keep it the same by rendering it unscathed and indeminified.

Derrida observes that such binding is crucial to civilizational identity, to the bonds of belonging and situating oneself: "whence the sense of 'scruple,' but also of choice, of reading, and of election, of intelligence, since there can be no selectivity without the bonds of collectivity and recollection,"[27] a paradox that bears on Beauvoir's understanding of the risk involved in every ethical choice. However, the logic of *différance* makes clear the impossibility of anything ever being utterly fixed, static, or definitively the same, alerting us to the "phantasmic" character of much that we revere and indemnify in our various practices, while attending to

---

26  Derrida, in contesting the metaphysics of Euro-Mediterranean philosophy, argues against the concept of "presence" and "self-presence" by revealing the machinery of *différance* at work. Derrida offers the figure of the phantasm and the fetish to think through those axiomatic figures operating in European thought "designed to master the ideological formation they designated," and which become, in a certain reading, the "law of the castle," the rule of "the father," the law of the household – e.g. "economy," etc., as well as the illusion of a fixed "self." These are examples of the Derridean figure of the drive to "gather" and "bind" into a totality, which is one of the two impulses of European metaphysics.

Derrida argues against a "pure" or essential self-presence: self-presence, traditionally proven by phonocentrism, or the phenomenon of the subject speaking to herself, is an illusion – a "phantasm, in that any speaking to itself is compromised both by the relation to others who first give me my language and by a structure of *différance* that opens the purity of meaning to repetition and *différance*." In this analysis, the self speaks to itself in language provided by others and is thus already marked by another presence, which disturbs the phantasm of her inviolability. Moreover, in a deft but obvious observation, Derrida recasts writing as "trace," the marking that even as it repeats words leaves a remainder that exceeds the stroke, so that the words that the self repeats are always already iterable. The phenomenon or appearance of the purity of the "self," the sovereignty of the self who would *vouloir dire* in *Speech and Phenomena*, "is thus an effect of *différance*, not that which precedes and commands it," with the result that the concept of self-presence is a phantasm, and by inference, so is the sovereignty of the self. See Naas, "Comme Si, Comme Ça," 6.

27  Derrida, "Faith and Knowledge," 74.

the movement of this logic, which Derrida calls dissemination, the play of resistance and repetition.

The "religion" of the Roman Empire and its descendants gathers and binds meaning, practice, and power in various iterations. The term originally applied to adherents of a particular practice, an initially Christian practice. As Christianity became the official religion of the Holy Roman Empire, and by extension, European imperialism and capitalism, its tropes continue to inflect that empire's descendants – the technocracy of contemporary global capitalism:

> In this very place, *knowledge and faith, technoscience ("capitalist" and fiduciary) and belief, credit trustworthiness, the act of faith will always have made common cause, bound to one another by the band of their opposition*. Whence the aporia – a certain absence of way, path, issue, salvation – and the two sources.[28]

To the extent that the structure of this religion, or at least religiosity, continues to make "common cause" in the globalatinized world, it is fair to say, as Michael Naas observes, that there is no return to the religious since there can be no turning away from its play.[29] Derrida acknowledges that he is not able to

> undertake here all the analyses required by distinctions that are indispensable but rarely respected or practiced. There are many of them (religion/faith, belief; religion/piety; religion/cult; religion/theology; religion/theiology; religion/ontotheology; or yet again, religious/divine-mortal or immortal; religious/sacred-saved-holy-unscathed-immune-*heilig*). But among them, before or after them, we will put to the test the quasi-transcendental privilege we believe ourselves obliged to grant the distinction between ...[30]

That is, he can only here put to the test the distinction between faith and knowledge, the tension and play they involve and iterate today in an unprecedented movement, which Derrida calls *autoimmunity*, a mechanical, automatic movement in the scene of religion that

> is contradictory and distracting, both accessible, disconcerting and familiar, *unheimlich*, uncaany .... the double movement of abstraction and attraction that *at the same time detaches from and re-attaches to* the country, the idiom,

---

28 Derrida, "Faith and Knowledge," 43.
29 Naas, *Miracle and Machine*, 30.
30 Derrida, "Faith and Knowledge," 72.

the literal,or to everything confusedly collected under the terms "identity," and "identitarian ..."[31]

Here he observes the extent to which "religion" is both embedded in the social, poliitcal and economic matrix that is also called culture, at the same time that it is a force for gathering and identity, and of violent separation. Derrida illustrates this force, in the strange alliance of contemporary so-called fundamentalist Christian communities of the United States with the "lights" of the *tele-techno* – literally the light of our televisions and digital screens so deeply implicated in the reproduction of capitalist consumerism. This technology, product of the technocratic science whose effects – like abortion or stem-cell research – these communities reject, enables them to spread their message, which is the interpretation of the tradition they are trying to keep holy and indeminified, even as they engage the tools of that which threatens it. Derrida calls this movement an "enemy of life in the service of life,"[32] because it demands an absolute respect and reverence for life that often, and often in the three Abrahamic monotheisms, also demands the sacrifice of a life. It is a stance that produces the absurd proposition that life is only valuable if it is worth more than life, a stance that produces as a contemporary consequence the madness that Derrida decries, the distortion, torture or even annihilation of situated lives in the name of such an anomoly.

Although Derrida acknowledges the breadth of what the interrogation of religion requires, and reflects a sensitivity to the critical approaches of contemporary scholarship, within the constraints of his text, he can only unfold the structure of the religious "at the limit of reason," which is double:

> *on the one hand*, the experience of belief (trust, trust-worthiness, confidence, faith, the credit accorded the *good faith of the utterly* other in the experience of witnessing) and, *on the other*, the experience of sacredness, even of holiness, of the unscathed that is safe and sound (*heilig*, holy). These comprise two distinct sources or foci. "Religion" figures their *ellipse* because it both comprehends the two foci, but also sometimes shrouds their irreducible duality in silence, in a manner precisely secret and *reticent*.[33]

---

31  Derrida, "Faith and Knowledge," 78.
32  Derrida, "Faith and Knowledge," 84.
33  Derrida, "Faith and Knowledge," 72.

Religion, here, is thus both the experience of that which shall be indemnified, protected, made safe and sound, *heilig*, holy and, on the other hand, that faith which according to Derrida is the originary faith required in all human relations, the faith that proceeds from the promise to tell the truth to the other, and the other's faith in that promise, even when that promise is false or fails. This faith, he carefully notes, "*has not always been and will not always be identifiable with religion, nor, another point, theology. All sacredness and holiness are not necessarily, in the strict sense of the term, if there is one, religious.*"[34] He further observes that these two foci, faith and knowledge, do not belong to any determinate religion, (granting that the word religion only "properly" refers to Christianity).[35] In this, Derrida identifies an opening in the ellipse called religion, an opening through faith. This faith, because it exceeds the limits of determinate religion, provides an opening in the machine that at present renders the religion of the imperial-capitalist-technological hegemony "breathless," without "respiration," and therefore, ironically, without "spirit."[36] It is this iteration of faith, and its impossible relation to knowledge, that informs my reading of Beauvoir's ethic in Chapter Four.

Derrida is also, like Beauvoir, alert to the seductiveness of "knowledge," that absolute, transcendent intelligibility that is proffered as the light of truth in which one should believe:

> The temptation of knowing, the temptation of knowledge is to believe not only that one knows what one knows (which wouldn't be too serious) but also that one knows what knowledge is, that is, free, structurally, of belief or of **faith** – of the fiduciary or of trustworthiness. The temptation to believe in knowledge, here for example in the precious authority of Benveniste, can hardly be separated from a certain fear and trembling.[37]

---

34 Derrida, "Faith and Knowledge," 48.
35 Derrida, "Faith and Knowledge," 72.
36 Here, Derrida is playing on the etymology of "breath," which, in many languages – Hebrew, Greek, Latin – is the same word for "air," "wind," and "spirit." See Hebrew *ruach*; Greek *pneuma*; Latin *spiritus*.
37 Derrida "Faith and Knowledge." 68. Derrida has consulted the etymological texts of Benveniste throughout as a starting point for reflecting on the powerful language of "religion," as well as to critique the instability of his certainties, a great scholar "who walks with a tranquil step as though he knew what he was talking about, while at the same time acknowledging that at bottom he really doesn't know very much."

Here Derrida evokes the Greek (and Latin) traditional account of knowledge, knowledge as that which is beyond time and change, eternal and absolute Forms, always accessible to the intelligence by virtue of inhabiting the intelligible realm. This account of knowledge, foundational to the tradition of "Western" metaphysics (if not all metaphysics) is the subject of much modern philosophical contestation, beginning with Schoepenhauer, made operatic in Neitzsche, and methodically undermined in Derrida. Knowledge occupies a place in the entire chain of metaphysical claims which privileges the concept of presence, permanence, stasis, eternity and all those adjacent binaries of male/female; mind/body; spirit/matter; heaven/earth; ergo, knowledge/faith or faith/knowledge. Knowledge *is* the *heilig*, the holy, that which is indeminifed, as these are its necessary conditions.

Having identified the two sources of religion, Derrida examines a chain of doublings at work in religion, an examination required by the logic of *différance* he is following. This complex deconstructive reading of "religion in the singular," by which he intends to argue that there is a singular structure of "religiosity," has and will continue to require careful reflection and explication. But at the heart of this structure is the powerful claim: "Religion is *the response*."[38] This formula evokes both the specific Latin European history of religion as well as its performative structure, the script that has been played since the Roman moment, and which continues to be performed in this current global moment, this *"strange alliance of Christianity, as the experience of the death of God, and teletechnoscientific capitalism."*[39]

> What does it mean to say that religion is the response?
> No response, indeed, without a principle of responsibility: one must respond to the other, before the other and for oneself. And no responsibility without a *given word*, a sworn faith <*foi jurée*>, without a pledge, without an oath ...[40]

This formula introduces the critical roles required in this scene: self-other, self-to-oneself, and their movement – the movement of appeal and response. The other in question is not necessarily the Other that is also called the One; in fact, Derrida explicitly links all "others" as equal in their singularity, equal in their appeal: *"tout autres est tout autres."*[41] The other

---

38  Derrrida, "Faith and Knowledge," 64.
39  Derrrida, "Faith and Knowledge," 52.
40  Derrrida, "Faith and Knowledge," 64.
41  Derrrida, "Faith and Knowledge," 69.

– any other, each other that one might respond to, not necessarily or only the Other traditionally signified by "God" – is the focus of *The Gift of Death*, the text I now detour through in order to examine this play of response.

*The Gift of Death* argues that the history of "religion" is also the history of the "self."[42] It is significant that Derrida reads two 19th century writers, Kierkegaard and Baudelaire, in addition to the 20th century philosopher Patocka, settling his reflections on the self as it is defined, post-Enlightenment. He reviews Patocka's account of how the pre-Platonic "demonic" and "orgiastic" mysteries are incorporated into Platonism, and then into the Christian *mysterium tremendum*, by which the incorporated orgiastic and demonic are repressed. For Derrida, the point of interest is the play of both forces:

> Religion is responsibility or it is nothing at all. Its history derives its sense entirely from the idea of a passage to responsibility. Such a passage involves traversing or enduring the test by means of which the ethical conscience will be delivered of the demonic, the mystagogic, and the enthusiastic, of the initiatory and the esoteric. In the authentic sense of the word, religion comes into being the moment that the experience of responsibility extracts itself from that form of secrecy called demonic mystery.[43]

The demonic is pre-responsible, as it "belongs to a space that does not yet resound with the injunction to respond, a space in which one does not yet hear the call to explain oneself [*répondre de soi*], one's actions, or one's thoughts, to respond to the other and answer for oneself before the other."[44] This "demonic mystery" both precedes and composes the self understood as singular situated autonomous person, to the extent that its desire for "absolution" is only possible from the position of emerging self-consciousness. The demonic desire for absolute union, for a losing of oneself in the other by means of the other, to become literally "enthused," recalls Beauvoir's observation that this yearning is self-defeating, in that if realized it would render the world airless, spaceless, and horizonless in its totalizing force.[45] These demonic remains, at play in the culture we inherit, also pose the risk of making responsibility to an other impossible by negating its conditions: the condition where self responds to other.

---

42 *The Gift of Death* is primarily structured according to Derrida's reading of the philosopher Jan Patocka, although it detours into Kierkegaard, Baudelaire and the Gospel of Matthew.
43 Derrida, *The Gift of Death*, 5.
44 Derrida, *The Gift of Death*, 5.
45 Beauvoir, *Pyrrhus and Cineas*, 126; and *The Prime of Life*, 477–78.

The demonic seeks the homogeneity of ecstatic union, where "one does not resound with the injunction to respond." Derrida, regarding Patocka's account of the emergence of "religion" out of the Greco-Roman-European context, notes that this,

> will overlap with the genealogy of the subject who says "myself," the subject's relation to itself as an instance of liberty, singularity, and responsibility, the relation to self as being before the other; the other in its infinite alterity, one who gives without being seen but also whose infinite goodness gives in an experience that amounts to the gift of death [*donner la mort*]. For the moment, let's leave the expression in all its ambiguity.[46]

To the extent that responsibility must be located in a singular individual conscience, and to the extent that Christianity involves the self in a relation to another before whom we must respond and be responsible, "The history of responsibility is tied to a history of religion."[47] He argues that history is itself inextricably bound to responsibility, to faith and to the gift:

> To responsibility in the experience of absolute decisions that involve breaking with knowledge or given norms, made therefore through the very ordeal of the undecidable; to religious faith through a form of involvement with or relation to the other that is a venture into absolute risk, beyond knowledge and certainty; to the gift and to the gift of death that puts me in relation with the transcendence of the other – with God as selfless goodness – and that gives me what it gives me through a new experience of death. Responsibility and faith go together, however paradoxical that might seem to some, and should, in the same movement, exceed mastery and knowledge. The gift of death would be this marriage of responsibility and faith.[48]

The "gift of death" is multivalent. It is the awareness in each individual of her own mortality, and of the irreplaceable singularity of her own death to the extent that the individual bears the weight of her choices, her projects. In a passage reminiscent of Beauvoir,[49] he explains,

> Because I cannot take death away from the other who can no more take it away from me in return, it remains for everyone to take his own death upon himself. Everyone must assume their own death, that is to say, the one thing

---

46 Derrida, *The Gift of Death*, 5.
47 Derrida, *The Gift of Death*, 7.
48 Derrida, *The Gift of Death*, 8.
49 Beauvoir, *Pyrrhus and Cineas*, 11.

in the world that no one else can either give or take: therein resides freedom and responsibility.⁵⁰

Therein resides "freedom and responsibility" because in assuming one's own death, one assumes the finitude of one's existence, and therefore the weight of responsibility for one's choices. "In this sense, only a mortal can be responsible",⁵¹ as only a mortal bears the weight of that specific finitude.

The "gift of death" is also "putting to death," as well as giving oneself or an other death. Derrida's considers Kierkegaard's treatment of Abraham's sacrifice of Isaac and the links Kierkegaard makes between this and Christianity. Derrida describes his rendering of this scene, in which,

> We fear and tremble because we are already in the hands of God, although free to do work, but in the hands and under the gaze of God, whom we don't see and whose will we cannot know, no more than the decisions he will hand down nor his reasons for wanting this or that, our life and death. We fear and tremble before the inaccessible secret of a God who decides for us although we remain responsible, that is to say free to decide, to work, to assume our life and death.⁵²

Derrida argues for the double impulses of "passion" and responsibility in response to the "unseen gaze" of one who is unknowable, and who therefore is the condition for one's decision: one responds in risk and "fear and trembling." "Passion" refers to the Platonic incorporation of demonic mystery, where the responsibility is directed toward the *mysterium et tremendum* of Christianity, the Platonic form of the Good now become a persona, an object of desire – eros – that represses (thus repeats) the demonic mystery. Here, as in "Faith and Knowledge," Derrida names the possibility of a discourse on "religion without religion" which he calls the "non-determined." At the same time, this discourse is also an examination of European responsibility that can only be Christian:

> On what condition is responsibility possible? On the condition that the Good no longer be a transcendental objective, a relation between objective things, but the relation to the other, a response to the other; an experience of personal goodness, and a movement of intention.⁵³

---

50 Derrida, *The Gift of Death*, 45.
51 Derrida, *The Gift of Death*, 42.
52 Derrida, *The Gift of Death*, 57.
53 Derrida, *The Gift of Death*, 51.

Responsibility requires, structurally, a relationship between persons, between "points of view," a requirement the abstract Platonic Form of the Good cannot fulfill. The person involved in Kierkegaard's fable is the One who calls Abraham, the same One who sacrifices "his" only son in the gospel narratives. This particular scene of an unseen unknowable Absolute Other, whose gaze establishes my "self," and whose gaze demands response – to secretly and without calculation sacrifice the one who is most beloved – is found in the story of Abraham and Isaac, and repeated in the Christian narrative of the Passion of Jesus the Christ. Describing the Absolute Other in the Christian narrative as an instance of "infinite love," he asks,

> On what condition does goodness exist beyond all calculation? On the condition that goodness forgets itself, that the movement is the movement of the gift that renounces itself, hence a movement of infinite love. Only infinite love can renounce itself and, in order to *become finite*, become incarnated in order to love the other, to love the other as a finite other. This gift of infinite love comes from someone and is addressed to someone; responsibility demands irreplaceable singularity. Yet only death, or rather the apprehension of death, can give this irreplaceability, and it is only on the basis of that one can speak of the responsible subject, of the soul as conscience of self, of myself, etc.[54]

The inference in this observation is that the requirement for irreplaceability – the irreplaceability of the singular situated self – may be absent in the appeal of the One who is also the person of Infinite love, an aporia for further reflection. At the same time, in describing a most determinate scene of "religion" here, Derrida visits the same figures that inhabit the existential perspective: the consciousness of finitude, which is the field of decision, and the response to the other on the basis of this finitude, on the basis of the singularity granted by "the gift of death." In this Euro-Christian reading, one that echoes Kant's "good without qualification," responsibility is "to respond as oneself and as irreplaceable singularity, to answer for what one does, says, gives; but it also requires that, being good and through goodness, one forgets or effaces the origins of what one gives."[55]

The "origins of what one gives" is highlighted in the case of Abraham and the sacrifice of Isaac. In Derrida's reading, the story of Isaac is a

---

54 Derrida, *The Gift of Death*, 51.
55 Derrida, *The Gift of Death*, 52.

"nocturnal mystery" of which, if we can speak of it at all, is "abominable" and at the same time, "also the most common thing:"

> Duty or responsibility binds me to the other, to the other as other, and binds me in my absolute singularity to the other as other. God is the name of the absolute other as other and as unique (the God of Abraham defined as the one and unique). As soon as I enter into a relation with the absolute other, my singularity enters into a relation with his on the level of obligation and duty. I am responsible before the other; I answer to him and I answer for what I do before him. But of course, what binds me thus in my singularity to the absolute singularity of the other immediately propels me into the space of risk or absolute sacrifice. There are also others, an infinite number of them, the innumerable generality of others to whom I should be bound by the same responsibility, a general and universal responsibility (which Kierkegaard calls the ethical order). I cannot respond to the call, the request, the obligation, or even the love of another without sacrificing the other other, the other others. Every other (one) is every (bit) other [*tout autre est tout autre*]; everyone else is completely or wholly other. The simple concepts of alterity and singularity constitute the concept of duty as much as that of responsibility. As a result, the concepts of responsibility, of decision, or of duty, are condemned, a priori to paradox, scandal and aporia.[56]

It is clear that this play between the self and the other – as a play of appeal and response – can be read in all other relationships, in all other situations of appeal and response, situations that are at the same time unique and singular. Speaking specifically of Abraham, who could not speak about his duty to the Absolute, Derrida observes the double movement: on the one hand, obeying his duty to the God he must love above all else, which founds his responsibility – his answering for himself before God; on the other hand, because bound by secret command, he must sacrifice the person he loves most in the world, his only son, and so be seen as irresponsible and unethical in the eyes of his fellow human beings.

From this aporia, Derrida reads the inevitable logic of responsibility, that it always requires the sacrifice of someone. Every singularity before whom we are answerable excludes all the other possible singularities and thus, all responsibility is "condemned, a priori." Nothing can "justify" the choice of this singularity rather than that one: at the same time, "we also do our duty by behaving thus."[57] Sacrifice always already involves an inherent sacrifice in the choice of whom we respond to, in addition

---

56 Derrida, *The Gift of Death*, 69.
57 Derrida, *The Gift of Death*, 71.

to any injunction we obey for the other. The inference of sacrificing for the "one who sees in secret," in whose "unseen gaze" you are held, is that this is performed at the expense of the living warmth across from you, the other person whose gaze you receive and return, recognizing and being recognized. This is the cost of responsibility to the phantasm named "God," to exchange that person whose gaze you can return for one whose gaze remains invisible. Even if the relationship is between persons who see one another, there is still the fact of sacrifice in the response to the appeal: when I respond to this one, I have sacrificed all the others. This is remarkably close to Beauvoir's observation of the same aporia in *Pyrrhus and Cineas* and in *The Ethics of Ambiguity*, the ambiguity that "working for some often means working against others,"[58] an ambiguity without resolution, but one which is not an excuse for inaction. She observes that each individual is bound to all others as a condition of meaning, a condition that is "precisely the ambiguity of his condition: in surpassing toward others, each one exists absolutely as for himself; each is interested in the liberation of all, but as a separate existence engaged in his own projects."[59] From this she concludes that "in order to serve some men we must do disservice to others."[60] This gives rise to the ethical question, "by what principle do we choose between them,"[61] and while such a principle is duly explored in her ethic, the fact of all response to the other entailing sacrifice is maintained, which is the aporia of responsibility before a singularity.

Linking the scene of Abrahamic (and therefore Christian) responsibility to the tele-techno-capitalist regime, Derrida asks whether the sacrifice of Isaac is not "the most common event in the world," due to the "the structure of the laws of the market" that,

> allows to die of hunger and disease tens of millions of children (those relatives or fellow humans that the ethics or the discourse of the rights of man refers to) without any moral or legal tribunal ever being considered competent to judge such sacrifice, the sacrifice of the other to avoid being sacrificed oneself. Not only does such a society participate in this incalculable sacrifice, it actually organizes it.[62]

Here, we are given the example of how choosing one involves sacrificing others. If we accept Derrida's account, wherein the Christian, emerging

---

58   Simone de Beauvoir, *Pyrrhus and Cineas*, 127.
59   Simone de Beauvoir, *The Ethics of Ambiguity*, 112.
60   Simone de Beauvoir, *The Ethics of Ambiguity*, 113.
61   Beauvoir, *The Ethics of Ambiguity*, 113.
62   Derrida, *The Gift of Death*, 86.

from the Platonic and Abrahamic, incorporates and represses the double injunction of responsibility – pure passion and duty before the other – now he will draw the line connecting the Greco-Roman-Christian and the tele-techno-capitalist. The contemporary order is "founded upon a bottomless chaos (the abyss or open mouth),"[63] one that speaks,

> a lexicon concerning responsibility that can be said to hover vaguely about a concept that is nowhere to be found, even if we won't go so far as to say that it doesn't correspond to any concept at all. It amounts to a disavowal whose resources, as one knows, are inexhaustible.[64]

Those who dare to "avow" the absence of true responsibility (for example, Derrida) on behalf of this "order" founded on the "open mouth" are treated as "nihilist, relativist, even poststructuralist, or worse, deconstructionist, all those who remain concerned in the face of such a display of good conscience."[65]

He implies we should not be surprised at this, because the economy of the present order, which can be read as the demands of profitability requiring the sacrifice of tens of millions of children, is itself an iteration of a certain economy of sacrifice that Derrida reads in Christian theology. Reflecting on *Matthew* 5, Derrida observes the language of "profit," "sacrifice" and "reward:"

> the question of remuneration will permeate the discourse on God the father who sees in secret and who will reward you (by implication with a salary). We need to distinguish between two types of salary: one of retribution, equivalent exchange, within a circular economy; the other of absolute surplus value, heterogeneous to outlay or investment ...[66]

The suggestion here is that the structure of an "absolute" authority engaged in an economy of compensation – here "God" promising "compensation" in the hereafter – is the same structure at work in the global "economy" of capitalism: the absolute authority of "maximum sustainable profitability," expedited at the cost of the lives of the dispossessed, is obeyed and rewarded, or some, in the economy of equivalent exchange, for others, in the reward of surplus payment.

---

63 Derrida, *The Gift of Death*, 86.
64 Derrida, *The Gift of Death*, 85.
65 Derrida, *The Gift of Death*, 85.
66 Derrida, *The Gift of Death*, 105.

"Religion" as "response" in its specific emergent context is also a play of conscience and consciousness. God the father, part of the chain of metaphysical absolutes – "Spirit," "Law," "Eternity," etc – who "sees in secret," enjoins us to respond, to do our duty. Hence, God inaugurates the scene of sacrifice and its inevitable guilt, as well as the aporia of being responsible – in secret – and at the same time we appear irresponsible to others. Derrida goes so far as to suggest we abandon "idolatrous" concepts of God as "over there," and instead conceive of the one to whom we pledge as the "self," our own self:

> we might say: God is the name of the possibility I have of keeping a secret that is visible from the interior but not from the exterior. As soon as such a structure of conscience exists, of being-with-oneself, of speaking, that is to say of producing invisible sense, as soon as I have within me, thanks to the invisible word as such, a witness that others cannot see, and who is therefore at the same time other than me and more intimate with me than myself, as soon as I can have a secret relationship with myself and not tell everything, as soon as there is secrecy and secret witnessing within me, and for me, then there is what I call God, (there is) what I call God in me (it happens that [*il y a que*] I call myself God – a phrase difficult to distinguish from "God calls me," for it is on such a condition that I can call myself or be called in secret. God is in me, he is the absolute "me" or "self," he is that structure of invisible interiority that is called, in Kierkegaard's sense, subjectivity ... That is the history of God and of the name of God as the history of secrecy, at the same time secret and without any secrets. Such a history is also an economy."[67]

Consonant with Patocka's thesis that the genealogy of "religion" is also the genealogy of "consciousness/conscience," here Derrida explicitly suggests that the "God who sees in secret" and to whom we respond can be read as our own interiority, our putative self-conscious "subjectivity." It is noteworthy that he does not use the ontological terminology in his analysis: that is, he does not say what "God" *is*: rather, he proposes what the sign "God" might name. This is significant because it respects the undecideability of the sign "god," recognizing that just because its iteration as an absolute static being is impossible according to the logic of *différance*, there may be other ways for the sign to operate, like the invisible "interiority" proposed above. As such, it produces the same economy of response and the same ethical aporia as that given in Kirkegaard's reading of the Abrahamic myth. Here is the same dynamic of Hegel's dialectic of consciousness, in which the self perceives itself as its own other: but we also

---

67  Derrida, *The Gift of Death*, 108.

see in this particular iteration the inference of both a "passion" or love beyond calculation, and of an economy of reward and debt that motivates the response.

This conception of God as the possibility of the "self" is, on the one hand, a rejection of metaphysics, a rejection of a transcendent almighty absolute. Such a rejection becomes possible in the recent moment of European civilization, the moment of Kierkegaard, Nietzsche, Freud and eventually Beauvoir. But even as this movement of rejection denies the God of metaphysics, and its indemnification, at the same time, the structure of the religious continues to operate to the extent that the possibility of this "self" Derrida reads as "God" is engaged in the play of responsibility: here, the self responding to itself as other. Such a revisioning of "mystical foundation of authority" expressed in the God of the European tradition can only occur within that tradition, as a response to that tradition and so as an iteration of that tradition.

Derrida concludes, in the face of today's "economy" and its sacrifices:

> One must keep in the gift only the giving, the act of giving, and the intention to give, not the given, which in the end doesn't count. One must give without knowing, without knowledge or recognition, without thanks (*remerciement*) without anything, or at least, without any object.[68]

We may note here the contrast between the Abraham and Isaac narrative and the *Matthew* text in question, a contrast that gives us two iterations of the Other to whom we respond. Abraham gives without knowing and without calculation, obliged to trust the One who calls him, in secret, with no promise of remuneration, and a demand for sacrifice. The gospel discourse about "God the father" promises remuneration, and with this entails the kind of calculation which Derrida argues alters and destroys the gift. The suggestion here is that the incorporation of the Platonic "Good," the gazeless form of the Good, into the Christian person of "God the father" bears within it a loss of generosity, as it also bears within it the chain of the "demonic" and "orgiastic" which, incorporated into the Platonic, is subsequently incorporated into the Christian: "it does not yet resound with the injunction to respond," even as the One as "father" enjoins us to "do our duty." Thus we are faced with another iteration of the aporia, that we must respond to the One who calls us to infinite love, even as the One is unmasked as a dealer or a banker in an economy of sacrifice. This "scene," as Derrida reads it in Patocka, emerging as it does from the particular

---

68 Derrida, *The Gift of Death*, 108.

## Setting the Scene 49

chain of the Greco-Judaic-Christian, is disseminated at the same time as the psychological drama of the contemporary "self."[69]

As we have seen, the idea of response is closely allied to the appeal of the other, and of the Absolute Other, the "other" whose truth it is tempting to "know," to make "holy." According to the logic of *différance*, the thing indemnified will escape, will exceed the boundaries of the "sacred" space, will find itself contaminated: it will not remain *heilig*, holy, unscathed, any more than the cell that exerts itself to ward off disturbance can avoid the disturbance it has caused itself. At the same time, it is not an option to *not* respond to the appeal of the other. As we have seen in the logic of sacrifice, it is only thus that we do our duty, and so we again are condemned to paradox, aporia, ambiguity.

In the light of this genealogy of the self and responsibility, let us return to "Faith and Knowledge" and Derrida's further reflection on faith as a source of religon. In an attempt to think abstractly the origins of religion, he names two sources again – provisionally: "*the messianic, or messianicity without messianism*" and "*chora,*" which cannot be formulated, which is "*radically heterogenous to the safe and sound, to the holy and the sacred, it never admits of any indeminification.*"[70]

The first "origin" for faith is the *messianicity without messianism*. The Hebrew figure of *messiah* denotes the annointed one, one who delivers from oppression, a term translated in Greek by *christos*. Derrida asks us to think messianicity not as belonging to any determinate tradition or prophetic announcement, but rather, linked to an "*invincible desire for justice,*" which we might understand as a persistent hope for justice that informs our promises to one another, to our acts of faith "*that inhabit every act of language and every address to the other.*"[71]

> *This justice, which I distinguish from right, alone allows the hope, beyond all "messianisms," of a universalizable culture of singularities, a culture in which the abstract possibility of an impossible translation could nevertheless be announced. ... This messianicity, stripped of everyhting, as it should, this faith without dogma which makes its way through the risks of absolute night, cannot be contained in any traditional opposition, for example that between reason and mysticism.*[72]

---

69 This is the main scaffold of Derrida's analysis of Patocka, most explicitly stated in *The Gift of Death*, 7–9.
70 Derrida, "Faith and Knowledge," 58.
71 Derrida, "Faith and Knowledge," 58.
72 Derrida, "Faith and Knowledge," 56.

This paradoxical figure of messianicity brings us to the present play of the scene of religion. Derrida proposes "a universalizable culture of singularities" as the recipients of this hope for justice. Here he honours that thinking given in Kant, that each person is "an end in himself," that is, unique, singular, finite by virtue of their mortality and, on the other hand, in this condition bonded to every unique singular other person. On the basis of this bond, predicated on singularity and difference, we can hope for justice in a "universalizable culture of singularities." It is also striking that this messianicity involves no static metaphysical truth or person, but is founded in "every address to the other," a condition at the heart of Beauvoir's ethic. As one of the sources of the faith that is itself a source of religion, Derrida acknowledges messianicity as a force of composition and annihilation: that the possibility of messianicity, "*in uprooting the tradition that bears it, in atheologizing it, this abstraction, without denying faith, liberates a universal rationality and the political democracy that cannot be dissociated from it.*"[73] Post-enlightenment, post-Nietzsche, post-theisms, Derrida's figure of messianicity redeems the play we are calling here religion, delivering it from the idolatry of metaphysics, in the openess to justice for a future culture of each and every one, a culture of response and responsibility that acknowledges its inherent paradox.

The other originary figure, one that he says precedes messianicity, one that precedes everything, is *chora* [sic].[74] Alluding to his reading of *Khora* in "Plato's Pharmacy," "Khora," and "Sauf le Nom," Derrida briefly suggests the indefinability of *chora* by relating it to abstract spacing, "to place itself,"[75] an aporetic figure for the origin of the originary, "*the immemoriality of a desert in the desert which is neither a threshold nor a mourning.*" It is here that the discourse about "revelation" and "revealability" are located. "Revealability" is a quality that transcends any particular tradition, and which implies the figure of the "secret," of a faithfulness to that which one cannot share, of an allegiance to some thing within, hidden, and thus "subjective" [only ever subjective]. At the same time, one wants to share this secret faithfulness, and make it binding to the other. This is the duality of "revelation:" the "light of truth" that emanates from a nocturnal place, as Naas reads it, "a nocturnal source that is based on the inaccessibility of

---

73 Derrida, "Faith and Knowledge," 57.
74 Derrida usually transliterates χωρα as *khora*, but in this text, translated by Samuel Weber, the choice was made to use "ch" for the *chi* rather than the more typical "kh."
75 Derrida "Faith and Knowledge," 57.

the other."⁷⁶ The secret is that one is inaccessible in her otherness, as is the other. Each one is linked to the other only by the cool hand of *fiabilité*, by the risk of faith. This is the origin of every social bond. Revelation is the performance of the social bond, where the originary faith that connects our contingencies to one another reveals precisely the otherness of each individual, and, at the same time, unites us in the bond of the promise, also called the *event* or "miracle." Derrida explains,

> There is no opposition, fundamentally, between "social bond" and "social unravelling." A certain interruptive unravelling is the condition of the "social bond," the very respiration of all "community." This is not even the knot of a reciprocal condition, but rather the possibility that every knot can come undone, be cut or interrupted. This is where the *socius* or the relation to the other would disclose itself to the secret of testimonial experience – and hence, of a certain faith.⁷⁷

This is space of the originary faith, where it founds all social relations, including those involved in science, technoscience, and economics, one that exceeds all determinate cultural traditions. He also makes clear that this faith inhabits every movement of the social, a double movement that teeters between bond and unravelling, a space of risk that compels faith. The figure of autoimmunity offers an analysis of this unstable space.

To illustrate autoimmunity at work in the contemporary iteration of religion, Derrida describes the example of the rise of the Fundamentalist Christian movement in the USA in recent decades. This example decries the moral peril of the contemporary technological context and its threat to "Christian values," even as it does so by means of the very technology produced by this same modernity. Christian Fundamentalists attempt to indemnify their "holy" and unassailable moral and social commitments through the use of a technology so ubiquitous in their lived experience, that this same technology conveys the "other" that they wish to escape, eroding the base of their resistance. Ironically, the science which produces this technology, the science which threatens the indemnified and uncritically held tenets of this movement, is itself in part founded on the same originary faith as religion: it too believes in the promise to tell the truth, even if the promise is unfulfilled.⁷⁸

---

76 Naas, *Miracle and Machine*, 87.
77 Derrida, "Faith and Knowledge," 99.
78 Derrida, "Faith and Knowledge," 82–83.

Derrida suggests that the condition of autoimmunity is everywhere that globalatinization is. The world held in the grasp of globalatinization inherits religion and its two sources, so that everywhere there arises the way of indemnification of a phantasm of sovereignty – "God," "God's Law," "Human Rights," etc. – always already accompanied by and in tension with the "un-way" of originary faith. The section called "Et grenades" offers a double reading of this figure. The word *grenade* is French for "pomegranate," a fruit that typically features in the Passover Seder of the Sephardim of Algeria. A grenade is also an incendiary weapon. Both connotations are present in this image: "Emblem of a still life: an opened pomegranate, one Passover evening, on a tray."[79] The image suggests the two sources of Religion, the promise that appeals to faith, given in the knowledge of the experience of that worth indemnifying, the "light of revelation." This image of that ancient Jewish ritual of remembrance gives a double reading: the Seder ritual evokes that pledge to a beloved memory protected through repetition; and yet, this act of indemnification is presented here as a "still life:" an act of mourning, of keeping things in their place. At the same time, there is "still life" in this image: the living act of faith out of which such a practice is an affect. However, if the attempt to indemnify loses sight of the faith which transcends all particular practice and its implicit contingency and risk, it may lead to that other kind of "grenade," such as we see in the various conflicts around the globalatinized world.[80] Derrida observes,

> This self-contesting attestation keeps the auto-immune community alive, which is to say open to something other and more than itself; The other, the future, death, freedom, the coming or the love of the other, the space and time of a spectralizing messianicity beyond all messianism. It is here that the possibility of religion persists: the *religious* bond (scrupulous, respectful, modest, reticent, inhibited) between the value of life, its absolute "dignity," and the theological machine, the "machine for making gods."[81]

---

79 Derrida, "Faith and Knowledge," 100.
80 In addition to a general analysis of the violence begotten in the autoimmune performance, Derrida ends his essay by invoking *Genet at Chatila*, a memoir of the most horrific violence committed against Palestinian refugees in Beirut.
81 Derrida, "Faith and Knowledge,"87. Naas and Baring both address the influence of Bergson, the source of the quotation "machine for making gods" on Derrida, although he never explicitly treats a text by Bergson, except very briefly in passing in "Faith and Knowledge."

The last sentence quotes Henri Bergson, an influence on both Beauvoir and Derrida. Perhaps Derrida wants us to consider the totalizing force of the *uni-verse*, the one turning, and how such a construct reproduces the tension of faith and knowledge. The very idea of oneness and totality (which is exposed as unstable by the logic of *différance*) underwrites the idea of knowledge and the knowable, Plato's eternal absolute forms, and this in turn reproduces the desire to indemnify and eventually petrify this "knowledge," to make it be still, the same, to "move no more!"

This passage insists that the two sources of religion are both the "machine for making gods" and "something other and more than itself," "the coming or the love of the other." It enables us to think "religion" in relation to Beauvoir's critique of her context, in her sensitivity to the temptations of "metaphysics" and the "serious," and her exhortation to accept and *think* ambiguity. The ambiguous figure of the *grenade* warns of the unavoidable process of self-contestation that, seeking to indemnify something, at the same time launches a movement towards instability: "no *weg* without *umweg*,"[82] and the unknown on the horizon.

This review of the "scene of religion" from this reading of Derrida's texts shows that it is a play of "ambiguity," seen in the language of undecideability, of autoimmunity, of *différance*. In these texts, this scene is both specific, involving singular persons located in a particular historical context, and indeterminate; the scene involves an appeal and a response, moved by desire and unconditional generosity and yet at the risk of a deadly calculability. The persons in this scene are singular and free and must act in their freedom, trusting the other, believing in the other without calculation; at the same time, one risks the freedom of the other and therefore meaning, in the attempt to ontologize remains, in the attempt to indemnify and make "holy." Taken together, the elements of this play are an inheritance, by which our "selves" are both constituted and enjoined to respond. An integral figure in his discussion of inheritance is that of *mourning*, a figure that also draws us closer to Certeau.

The figure of mourning is linked to the phantasm and the spectre. In *Spectres of Marx*, Derrida meditates on the first scene of Hamlet,[83] in which

---

82 Derrida, "To Speculate: On Freud," 354–55.
83 This is an interesting echo of a passage in Certeau, in which Certeau reflects on the figure of "absence" by observing that Hamlet's father's ghost "once became the law of the castle," (Certeau, "*The Mystic Fable*," 2) raising the possibility that Certeau's 1982 text, to which Derrida responded, resonates in Derrida's 1994 *Spectres of Marx*, which begins with a prolonged reflection on Hamlet's spectral father.

the ghost of Hamlet's father appears. The ghost, who sees but cannot be seen behind his visor, a figure Derrida names the "*visor-effect*,"[84] evokes the unseen gaze of the One in Derrida's account of the Matthew text in *The Gift of Death*. The ghost of Hamlet's father, the phantasm, is "the basis of which we inherit from the law,"[85] and because unseen, is that toward which we must have faith, that his figure addressing us is the one we believe it is, that it speaks truth. In approaching this "thing" that is neither here nor not here, he advises that mourning is always at work: "we will be speaking of nothing else," because it is the condition of knowledge.[86] According to this logic, knowledge is the attempt "to ontologize remains, to make them present," which is a case of being "caught up in the work of mourning but, as such, it does not yet think it."[87] To know is to know who and where, to have a clear and irrefutable location for the thing. It is to know where the "remains" are even though, ironically, "remains" are the one thing that cannot be fixed in place, like the hidden law of composition of every text that deserves to be called text. He offers this figure in explanation:

> One has to know [especially the Body] ... to know is to know who and where – to know whose body it really is and what place it occupies ... it is necessary (to know – to make certain) that in what remains of him, he remain there. Let him stay there and move no more![88]

Against Freud, who argues for the closure successful mourning brings, Derrida doubts this is possible: "mourning is interminable. Inconsolable. Irreconcilable."[89] Mourning is inescapable in as much as we must continuously mourn the impossibility of mourning, as there is no presence, no body, no place that remains constant: to mourn is to mourn the instability of what is and was, to mourn the phantasm of that which is now gone from us and which was never present in some fixable state.

At the same time, to mourn the phantasm – that is, to mourn the mutability of the indeminified, the very possibility of indemnification – is to leave an opening for that which may come, *l'avenir*, for that which is impossible, unconditional, perhaps for "messianicity."[90] Such an opening is

---

84 Derrida, *Spectres of Marx*, 6.
85 Derrida, *Spectres of Marx*, 7.
86 Derrida, *Spectres of Marx*, 9.
87 Derrida, *Spectres of Marx*, 9.
88 Derrida, *Spectres of Marx*.
89 Derrida *The Work of Mourning*, 143.
90 Derrida, "Faith and Knowledge," 56.

never toward the teleological, or it would already be a closure of thought. The opening of the "to come," of the impossible, the unconditional, is precisely to that which is yet unthought, unknown, which constitutes *the event* beyond any sovereignty, beyond stasis. It is openness to that which is, to inflect the metaphysical term, "transcendent." In existential terms, it is that toward which our "useless passion" yearns, a horizon for our desire.

## III. WANDERERS IN A STRANGE LAND

This figure of mourning is perhaps the most obvious intersection between Derrida's thinking on religion and Michel de Certeau's examination of mysticism. Certeau, who is both a reader of Derrida and a subject of Derrida's reading,[91] a systematic renegade, this "historian of alterity" reads the arising of the mystic tradition in Renaissance Europe as a response to the empty tomb, to the absent "One." At the same time, he reads the mystic as the drama of the dialectic of self-consciousness. In the epoch of the mystic, the self-conscious self emerges in resistance to the hegemony of the church and carries the inheritance of responding to the holy. This self has lost its presence, has been forced to acknowledge the absence of presence, and so is launched in a wandering, a wandering that eventually arrives in the existential moment.

Certeau offers a sustained reflection on the desire which Hegel suggests constitutes self-consciousness. At the same time, as a historian and philosopher, he locates this desire in the specific context of late Renaissance Europe. Certeau gives a specific situated historical reflection on the "self" which develops co-evally with "religion," and the problem of the absent other, a condition with both theological and psychological implications. The figure of the absent One marks the beginning of a recognition that there is not and cannot be a "one" without immediatley inferring a "+," a supplement or remainder that tempt us to "ontologize." The figure of absence suggests that, far from obeying the demand to "move no more," the dead continue to move, haunting us, appealing to us. Certeau characterizes the experience of this absence as follows:

> What should be there is missing. Quietly, almost painlessly, this discovery takes effect. It afflicts us in a region we cannot identify, as if we had been stricken by the separation long before realizing it. When the situation finds expression, it may still borrow the words of the Christian prayer: "May I not

---

91 Derrida "A Number of Yes," 118–33.

be separated from Thee." Not without Thee. *Nicht ohne.* But the necessary, having become the improbable, is in fact impossible. Such is the figure of desire. It is obviously a part of the long history of that *One,* the origin and metamorphosis of which so intrigued Freud. One sole being is lacking, and all is lacking. This new beginning orders a sequel of wanderings and pursuits. One suffers the pangs of absence because one suffers the pangs of the One.[92]

"Mourning" is implied in his choice of language: "afflict," "stricken," "suffers the pangs of absence." Such are the affects of mourning. That which is mourned is the *One* who "should be there," but who is not. This is also the vocabulary of desire: this desire for the One who eludes us, ordering a "sequel of wanderings and pursuit," an unending desire that recalls Beauvoir's discussion of the *"passion inutile."* Like Beauvoir, Certeau does not try to reconcile the aporia of longing for communion with the one, even as he accepts the absolute alterity of each person.

Certeau's treatment of the one both as absence and as the object of desire brings us close to Hegel again, and even closer to Derrida and Beauvoir. Like the apophasis of the mystics he studies, Certeau can only say *where* and *what* the "one" is not. His insistence on an "absence" as the locus of desire suggests the rejection of tradtonal metaphysical ontology, of Being, of presence, of absolutes. It suggests an acceptance of instability, of becoming, of play. According to such a premise, the mystics inaugurate an understanding that the direction of desire puts in motion a scene of wandering, a scene that emerges in the play of religion. At the same time, Certeau remains close to Hegel in affirming desire as the defining action of the self.[93]

Certeau locates the mystic at a crucial turn of the Christian European world, at the cusp of secularism in 16th and 17th centuries. *The Mystic Fable* traces the history of those mystics as a response of some disaffected faithful to the eroding of the sovereign Christian institution. The etymology of the word "response" is important here, inflecting both Derrida and Certeau, from the Latin, "re" - again; *"spondere"* - to pledge: to pledge again, to promise again. These mystics pledge again their faith to the empty tomb, to the absence of one who has been displaced. They do not know where to find the "one," but they do know what it is not: it is not this. Thus, they

---

92 Certeau, *The Mystic Fable*, 9.
93 See Sieps, and Pippin, both of whose recent studies emphasize this premise in Hegel's *Phenomenology of Spirit*, of desire as a figure that has been neglected in Hegel studies.

wander, rejecting the phantasms of the Church, mourning the impossibility of mourning, pledging *again* and, in so doing, echoing the figure of faith given in Derrida, faith which "exceeds, through its structure, all intuition, and all proof, all knowledge."[94] Certeau's reads the Mystic (the term he uses for the porous boundaries of the epoch and its performers) as a wandering after One who is not there, "a mourning" for One who is no longer to be found. He says of his study,

> One who is missing moves it to be written. The story continues to be written during travels through a country from which I'm away ... One suffers the pangs of absence because one suffers the pangs of the One.[95]

For Certeau, the past always remains Other to the present, and in this he draws the scholar in this present time close to the Mystics she studies. As Marian Füssel observes, "The other is for Certeau 'the phantasm of historiography, the object that it seeks, honors, buries.'"[96] She longs to "speak to it," to that which is not [and never has been in any appropriate way] present. Yet the longing persists. Certeau notes: "Hamlet's father's ghost becomes the law of the castle in which he was no longer present."[97] This echoes the drive of the Mystic practice, an unanswerable longing, a desire for that which is absent, and this is replicated in Beauvoir's attestation to her own unending desire for an absolute union.

Certeau wryly observes that the historiographical practice of reviewing the Mystic past is located in a tradition that began with the discovery of an empty tomb. The Church, when understood as the Body of Christ, sought for that which was absent through its practice, through its *mystikos* – closing the eyes, seeing beyond ocular vision. It subsequently required the sealing of the lips to the uninitiated and, later, it referred to the esoteric exegesis of scripture. Only when the "spoken word" of the "One" ceases to resonate does the Mystic become internalized, cut off from the Body of the Absent One, now relegated to a no-place of unsaying, a listening for the Word that does not come.[98]

---

94  Derrida, "Faith and Knowledge," 98.
95  Certeau, *The Mystic Fable*, 2.
96  Marian Füssel, "Writing the Otherness – The Historiography of Michel de Certeau SJ," *Spiritual Spaces: History and Mysticism in Michel de Certeau*, edited by Inigo Bocken (Leuven: Peeters Press, 2013).
97  Certeau, *The Mystic Fable*, 4.
98  Certeau, *The Mystic Fable*, 153.

In developing his analysis, he identifies four discourses within which to think the Mystic, to "square the Mystic circle" which always exceeds its interrogation: historiography, psychoanalysis, the Mystic Fable itself, and a link between "modern" Mystics and the emergence of a "new eroticism." His review of the contexts of the Mystic reveal that those whom we associate with the 16th and 17th century practice tended to emerge from social conditions of decline: impoverished nobility, dispossessed gentry caught in the great upheavals driving these societies toward the "secular," a secular that engenders a new eroticism. A practical consequence of this is that it provides an opening for women – traditionally identified as carnal, material, and emotional – in the otherwise masculine ecclesia, in which

> learned clerics became exegetes of womens' bodies, speaking bodies, living Bibles spread here and there in the countryside or in the little shops, ephemeral outbursts of the "Word" erstwhile uttered by the whole world. A humbled theology, after long having exercised its magistracy, expected and obtained from its other the certainties that had eluded it.[99]

In this context, Certeau wants to show a link between the arrival of the new erotic and the "manner of speaking" that characterizes the "modern" Mystics.[100] The source of the Word who is gone missing is now found in that other, literally woman – the other of man, spirit, reason – and her body, now read as text, reveals "certainties" that had previously eluded theology, certainties that now replace the privileged unattainable knowledge of the tradition with the gaze of the embodied lover.

The relevance of this criteria to Beauvoir requires some expansion. Certeau argues that this movement was no mere coincidence. Both sprang from a "nostalgia" connected with the progressive decline of God as One, as object of love. Both are equally the effects of separation.[101] This displacement or substitution of One for an other is part of a chain of production, of "maintaining some kind of relationship with presences that are all now vanishing, despite the replacement of the Missing One by an indefinite series" of others.[102] In the context of this chain, the ascent of the spiritualization of the erotic, manifested earlier in the Courtly Love Tradition, is measured by an equal descent in the currency of Church's orthodox spirituality: "Since the thirteenth century (courtly love, etc.) a gradual religious

---

99 Certeau, *The Mystic Fable*, 26.
100 Certeau, *The Mystic Fable*, 4–5.
101 Certeau, *The Mystic Fable*, 4.
102 Certeau, *The Mystic Fable*, 4.

demythification seems to be accompanied by a progressive mythification of love. The One has changed its site."¹⁰³ "God" is replaced by woman, the divine word replaced by the loved body.

This movement is strikingly at play in Beauvoir's chapter entitled "The Mystic" in *The Second Sex*. Here, she offers her own iteration of this analysis:

> Love has been assigned to woman as her supreme vocation, and when she addresses it to a man, she is seeking God in him: if circumstances deny her human love, if she is disappointed or demanding, she will choose to worship the divinity in God himself... The Beloved is always more or less absent; he communicates with her, his worshipper, in ambiguous signs; she only knows his heart by an act of faith ...¹⁰⁴

In this passage, Beauvoir argues that contemporary woman has been called to replace a response to the appeal of God with a response to an appeal of man, in which the man becomes the substitute for the god, and like the one, is largely absent. The "largely absent man," as assigned object of desire, replaces the authority of god, and offers the promise (but rarely delivers) of an earthly communion, a substitute for the absolute union desired. While Beauvoir relocates the play of the mystic response to her own time, its play echoes Certeau's account and appeals for further analysis.

Returning to the theme of substitutions for the One, Certeau claims they remain "as elusive as the vanishing God," and so organize a productivity in response to this persistent absence in two directions: on the one hand, "now proliferating conquests destined to fill an original lack, now returning to the principle of these conquests and wondering about the "vacancy" of which they are the effects."¹⁰⁵ He maintains that it is the experience of these "vacancies" that carried the Mystics of the 13th–17th century, in its "manner of speaking," tracing the "ambiguous passage from presence to absence," bearing witness to "the slow transformation of the religious setting into an amorous one, or of faith into eroticism," telling how the body, "touched" by desire, engraved, wounded, written by the other, replaced the revelatory didactic word."¹⁰⁶

---

103 Certeau, *The Mystic Fable*, 4.
104 Beauvoir, *The Second Sex*, 709.
105 Certeau, *The Mystic Fable*, 4.
106 Certeau, *The Mystic Fable*, 5. At the same time, in an apparent contradiction, their very practices, predicated on a longing for an absence, end up "producing an erzatz presence," making "true" Mystics "suspicious and critical of what passes for "presence." They defend the inaccessibility they confront."

The subject of the "body" is indeed the question that consumes the Mystic writers of the 17th and 18th centuries."[107] What constitutes the "body," they ask: a divine word "which also had a physical nature and value," a lover's body "which is no less spiritual and symbolic in erotic practice,"[108] a body as text or text as body, "engraved, wounded, written upon,"[109] a community of the faithful, the body of that "fabula" invented for the Mystic tradition, or a matrix of all of these? All of these iterations bear on that which the Mystic seeks; some of these reflections haunt the texts of Beauvoir, particularly the body as the site of transcendent desire. She insists that the individual be regarded as whole, and that the body as a site of experience be valorized. Moreover, her own "conversion" away from Roman Catholicism and toward existentialism was itself accompanied by an erotic maturation, offering a singular repetition of that movement of the mystic story.[110]

The "manner of speaking" devised in the mystic discourse develops certain conventions, according to Certeau's analysis. One in particular deserves treatment here, as it provides a genealogical link between the mystic practice, the Enlightenment assertion of "self," and Beauvoir's vision of the human being. "Mystic discourse itself had to produce the condition of its functioning as a language that could be spoken to others and to oneself,"[111] in their fragmented "Babel-like" context. The first convention to facilitate this communication is the *volo* – "I will," a practice that "erected places for speaking."[112] The preliminary condition for speaking required 1) a form of exclusive restriction [e.g. "an 'only,' a 'nothing but,' or a 'no one except'"],[113] and a "will," which "constituted the *a priori* knowledge could no longer supply."[114] As a performative verb, the *volo* establishes the form of the discourse, whether "I want nothing," or "I want only." The *volo* "is absolute, not bound by any precise determination. It was defined by the disappearance of its objects."[115] Certeau cites the major subject of his scholarship, Jean Joseph Surin, who characterizes the *volo* as

---

107 Certeau, *The Mystic Fable*, 80.
108 Certeau, *The Mystic Fable*, 5.
109 Certeau, *The Mystic Fable*, 4.
110 Beauvoir, *Memoirs of a Dutiful Daughter*.
111 Certeau, *The Mystic Fable*, 164.
112 Certeau, *The Mystic Fable*, 165.
113 Certeau, *The Mystic Fable*, 165.
114 Certeau, *The Mystic Fable*, 166.
115 Certeau, *The Mystic Fable*, 166.

'to form desire.' A desire 'bound to nothing,' he added. In this discourse, this forming of desire as the "I want," is a wanting that is not determined, in which "To want all" and 'to want nothing' coincide.[116]

The important point here is the primacy of the "I" in this discourse about willing, an "I" that we might trace back to Descartes and his epistemological turn, positing the self as the first ground of philosophy. The primacy of this "I" in the mystic discourse is an effect of that "self" whose development Derrida claims accompanies religion.

Certeau argues that the *volo* – the "I will" – inaugurates all discourse, positing,

> from the very beginning what will be repeated in mystic discourse by many other verbs (to love, to wound, to seek, to pray, to die, etc.), itinerant acts among actors who may be positioned at one moment as subjects, at another as objects. Who loves whom? Who prays to whom? Sometimes God, sometimes the faithful ... The *volo* then, as beginning and centre, vanishing point and keystone of mystic communication, is the operative principle (and a verb) that will exercise all language.[117]

We can draw a line between this indispensable convention of mystic discourse, and the play of religion we have been reading in Derrida. While Certeau is describing the play in its particularity in the late Renaissance, he is describing again a scene in which a willing self is responding to an appeal by an other: "itinerant acts among actors who may be positioned at one moment as subjects, at another as objects," in the service of faith and desire, unable to "Ontologize" the remains of the absent one while perpetually seeking for them. We also see the development of the self-conscious self that is implicit in the "I will" of the *volo*, the discrete willing self who will occupy Kant, Hegel and Kierkegaard in the next centuries.

This figures in Beauvoir's ethic. First, Beauvoir insists on the moral freedom of every individual, which infers the corresponding responsibility of every individual. Allowing that there are those who do not embrace their freedom, those who do assume their freedom, through the projects they launch, by their *will*, are also launching their appeal to others. Here, the will is, as Surin suggests, "to form desire," to take that desire Beauvoir acknowledges as integral to the human condition, and to launch

---

116 Certeau, *The Mystic Fable*, 169.
117 Certeau, *The Mystic Fable*, 170.

it at something.[118] The will of the individual also establishes the conditions for appeal and response, and therefore faith, the willingness to believe, to trust, even at the risk of deception or failure. At the same time that this will, as presented in Beauvoir, is contingently destined to projects, to appeals to others, it is also, ultimately, "bound to nothing" in that all of its objects are also contingent, finite, and evanescent. Finally, beyond Beauvoir specifically, the establishment of the *volo* as the erector of mystic discourse – the positing of the "I will" as the beginning and centre of this "manner of speaking" anticipates the truncated development of the "I will," as the sovereign autonomous subject in certain Enlightenment philosophies, the "self" whose emergence Derrida argues is coeval with the scene of religion.

Certeau's third "side of the square" compares the tropes of psychoanalysis to the function of Mystic practice, part of his more subtle agenda of arguing that we still inhabit the far shore of the Mystic landscape, a landscape Beauvoir also inhabits. In Certeau's comparison, the Mystic and psychoanalysis both emerge as a challenge to an intellectually bankrupt yet politically and socially powerful orthodoxy: psychoanalysis as a challenge to the Bourgeoisie; the Mystic as a challenge to Roman Catholic orthodoxy.[119] According to this analysis, both contest the status quo and creatively push the boundaries of insight; yet both end up being appropriated by the very bodies that they served to disrupt, a movement resonant of Derrida's "autoimmunity."

Finally, Certeau conceives the Mystic in light of the "Mystic Fable" itself – that the practice itself, a "manner of speaking," a thoroughly linguistic undertaking, created a "fabula" of the Mystic in establishing itself. It "creates" a Mystic tradition within which to situate itself: however, it "only assembles and orders its practices in the name of something that it cannot make into an object (unless it be a Mystical one)."[120] Inheriting the "self" inaugurated in the Abrahamic and Platonic moments, the mystic utterances take on,

> a new locus, that of the *I*, and by the operation of (*spiritual*) exchanges that made communication hinge upon the question of the subject, and also by all the procedures, rhetorical or poetic, capable of organizing a field of allocution per se.[121]

---

118 Beauvoir, *The Ethics of Ambiguity*, 11–26.
119 Certeau, *The Mystic Fable*, 8.
120 Certeau, *The Mystic Fable*, 77.
121 Certeau, *The Mystic Fable*, 161.

In the scene of the mystic, "the universe, be it compact or infinite, be it regulated by order or chance, is posited in principle as the vocabulary of a *dialogical* discourse between a *you* and an *I* that seek one another through language,"[122] a position which instantiates the scene of the self and other through discourse, in particular through writing.

This discourse is governed by procedures in which the circumstances of the utterance are as important as what is said,[123] given that this discourse is an *action,* specifically, a speech act. This act of the subject, "in a more discrete but insistent tradition"[124] is "marked by the "yes" – a "yes" as absolute as the *volo,* without objects, without goals."[125] Here the quality of the yes, a yes which exceeds knowledge, functions like Derrida's gift, and like Beauvoir's "lucid generosity," unconditionally. This affirmation,

> brings together separation and openness, the *No-Name of the Other* and the *Yes* of volition, absolute separation and infinite acceptance.
> *Gott spright nur immer Ja.*
> God always says only Yes [or: I am].[126]

Certeau reads this *"conversar"* not only as historical data, but as a space for the speaking subject, a space which "hollows out" the interiority of the self, and the dynamic between the desiring self and the absent other. This in turn infers that the scene of the mystic utterance is itself an iteration of the scene of religion, and in its proximity to Beauvoir, anticipates her arrival.

Certeau's concludes with a return to the space of his text. He observes

> He or she is Mystic who cannot stop walking and, with the certainty of what is lacking, knows of every place and object that it is not that; one cannot stay there nor be content with that. Desire creates an excess .... Given over to a nameless desire, he is a drunken boat. Henceforth this desire can no longer speak to someone. It seems to have become *infans*, voiceless, more solitary and lost than before, or less protected and more radical, ever seeking a poetic body or locus. It goes on walking then, tracing itself out in silence, in writing.[127]

---

122 Certeau, *The Mystic Fable*, 163.
123 Certeau, *The Mystic Fable*, 164.
124 Certeau, *The Mystic Fable*, 174.
125 Certeau, *The Mystic Fable*, 174.
126 Certeau, *The Mystic Fable*, 175. This passage is the text which engages Derrida in his essay, "A Number of Yes."
127 Certeau, *The Mystic Fable*, 299.

Certeau's analysis of the multivalent sources of the Mystic – historical, intellectual, psychological, philosophical – provides a structure by which to approach the "self" received and given in Beauvoir, who is also called to respond. Her discourse is a testament to such a desire, an endless unassuaged desire, and her philosophy accepts and embraces the "wandering," "*infans*," that it entails. Her rejection of religion, in its aspect as a knowledge to be indemnified, is accompanied by a commitment to "originary faith," in her existential ethics. Her "nameless desire" sees her lifelong seeking of a "poetic body or locus." Beauvoir turns away from Roman Catholic practice, from the received "serious" given by her situation, and turns toward an exploration of her freedom, and its responsibility. She turns toward an inter-subjectivity that, in its potential for reciprocity, will found the meaning of her existence, in response to the other.

Religion is the response: as such, it involves risk, the risk of false commitments, of impossible sovereignties, as well as salvation, if we allow for the possibility of being saved from nihilism and injustice. For Beauvoir, the ambiguity of the human condition – the desire for union with other who is absolutely other – does not exhaust the appeal of the other, nor the response of the one who inherits this. It does not exhaust the mystic sojourn. The scene of religion is an iteration of this contingent and ambiguous human scene, and the heart of Beauvoir's philosophy performs within it.

Chapter 3

# Beauvoir's Conversion

In her account of her French Roman Catholic childhood, Beauvoir describes a tradition in which her longing for an absolute union with an other arises. This desire for an object that is forever receding from view might be called, following Certeau's discourse on the mystic, a "mystic attraction" in that the object of the attraction is unseen, ineffable and absent. She also recalls her rejection of her Roman Catholic bourgeois culture, which initiates her conversion to existentialism. This chapter will review Beauvoir's discourse about her own piety and disaffection, noting the ways in which this iterates the scene of religion and the mystic performance within that scene. These texts also testify to the relocation of the concept of transcendence, in which it ceases to refer to an untenable metaphysical condition, instead redeployed as a performative category in her existential scaffolding. Transcendence, as a function of existence, will provide the conditions necessary for faith and the meaning which accrues to it in her ethics of ambiguity.

Beauvoir's texts bear witness to her own experience of something that she wished to reproduce, a recurring experience that she deems "mystic," an impossible desire which results in relocating faith. Her *"passion inutile"* for an absolute union, a dissolving of the self into the another leads to her prolonged reflection on the relationship between I and Other. She reconsiders this desire, moving it away from the determinate tradition of French Catholicism to another site, the site of the ethics of ambiguity.[1] A review of

---

1   As noted earlier, Amy Hollywood, who has also written on Certeau in "Love Speaks Here: Michel de Certeau's *Mystic Fable*," reviews Beauvoir's discourse on the "mystics," as well as her attraction to mysticism. However, Hollywood does

her early fiction, *When Things of the Spirit Come First*, her autobiographies, *Memoirs of a Dutiful Daughter, The Prime of Life, Force of Circumstance: I and II, All Said and Done*, as well as her celebrated novel, *The Mandarins*, and her groundbreaking study, *The Second Sex*, provide a coherent testament to the depth of her youthful piety, the rigor of her rejection of the tradition she receives, and her careful exploration of the implications of the existential stance. In this redirecting of the faith she once aimed toward the divine, we see the operation of faith as that which exceeds determinate sites, as that which founds all relationships. Her rejection of her tradition and her embrace of atheism re-aligns the faith and knowledge that are the source of the scene of religion, rather than abrogates them.

Beauvoir's descriptions of her "religious" experiences resonate with the tropes of the mystic proposed by Certeau. In many ways, even the material and intellectual circumstances that enable and define the mystic discourse of the 16th and 17th centuries are repeated in the particular circumstances of Beauvoir's context, a repetition which helps to confirm the continuation of the broader scene of religion in which the mystic discourse, perhaps, continues. If one reads Beauvoir as inhabiting and resisting the hegemony of her situation, like the mystics of the 16th and 17th centuries, then Certeau's explication of the mystic moment illuminates Beauvoir's experience of that ambiguous something that cannot be bound, a something that is the source of endless desire. In spite of Beauvoir's many reflections about "religion," including mysticism, these figures, as they appear in her texts, are uninterrogated. Beauvoir assumes that religion – in particular, the bourgeois French Roman Catholic tradition – and mysticism refer to self-evident things. We will approach Beauvoir's treatment of religion and mysticism at face-value for the time being, as an entry into the larger scene. At the same time, the theoretical premise of this study – that Beauvoir inhabits the scene of religion, that play of faith and knowledge, promise and reproduction, self and other – is the enveloping context for this review of Beauvoir's conversion to existentialism.

Beauvoir's texts attest that the early 20th century socio-economic hegemony of bourgeois France is abetted by a Roman Catholic institution that has been assigned the task of disciplining the thoughts and

---

not offer a critical framework for her treatment of "religion" or "mysticism," treating both as self-evident categories of discourse. Eliane Lecarme-Tabone's insight – that Beauvoir's account of her rejection of her tradition inverts the terms of Pascal's wager – although also lacking a theoretical account of "religion," points in the direction of a relocation of the tropes of "religion" that I am developing here.

actions of its charges. However, while Beauvoir inherits the assumptions of the European Enlightenment, assumptions about the self as rational, autonomous subject, she is also moved to a state of wonder and ecstasy by the Other she meets through the Church. In these two very different turns of the religious, one in which she initially indemnifies the knowledge afforded in the rational Enlightenment ideals, the other in which she makes holy the One who is the truth and the light of the Catholic story, she performs a repetition of the tension between faith and knowledge in the scene of religion, and its annihilating effects on the church and society that have harbored them.

The following account of Beauvoir's conversion to existentialism will proceed, on the whole, chronologically in order of production: from her earliest fiction, *When Things of the Spirit Come First*, to her final autobiography, *All Said and Done*. They reveal a consistent and very self-conscious witnessing of the ambiguities that inform her philosophy: an impossible longing for union with an Absolute by a subject whose existence is governed by the finality of mortality; a desire for an experience of transcendence while admitting only the possibility of earthly delights; a longing for "being" even while acknowledging the absence of "Being." From her adolescence onward, Beauvoir consciously and thoughtfully rejects what she terms the "serious" cultural values of her bourgeois upbringing in the early 20th century , even as she reports with a bemused honesty the persistence of the attitudes and impulses that had once driven her to seek divine union. This coherence in her experience may be read as a turning of what Derrida calls the logic of "auto-immunity:" the endless desire for union with the other persists after her conversion to existentialism, undoing the first site in favor of another site. This move paradoxically serves to undermine the holiness of the orthodoxy that gave rise to this desire in the first place, thus the product of this orthodoxy – the mystic attraction – serving to attack the very system which produces it and which she was originally bound to defend. These texts also show that her attraction to what she terms mysticism, one which continues after her conversion to an existentialist philosophy, remains entirely consistent with the reading of the mystic offered by Certeau.

Between 1934 and 1938, Beauvoir undertook her first work of fiction, five loosely connected stories, each focusing on a young woman whose life in some way has been circumscribed and distorted by the constraints of bourgeois French Catholic values. Never published until 1972, this collection, *When Things of the Spirit Come First*, narrates the experience of five protagonists who either reject their bourgeois culture or are consumed by it. It is here that Beauvoir first inscribes her own watershed experience of losing faith in the Roman Catholic church and challenging the expectations of her social class. In the story, "Marcelle," we are told: "She stopped believing in god: with the immensity of human suffering before her, she felt quite sure that Providence did not exist."[2] The story, "Marguerite," narrates almost verbatim the same experience of "mysticisim" that Beauvoir later recounts in her autobiography. The protagonist explains how,

> I certainly had a natural aptitude for the mystic life; I would often lock the lavatory door and whip myself with a little gold chain; I also rubbed my thighs with pumice stone, which made red places that Mama dressed with ointment. The Abbe Mirande allowed me to take Communion three times a week and I made my confession to him every fortnight. He told Mama I had a beautiful soul …The older I grew, the greater my love of God became, but less and less did I think of sin …[3]

This passage echoes the account given in *Memoirs of a Dutiful Daughter*, published nearly nine years later. In the autobiographical reflection, she describes a wrenching epiphany about her actual confessor, Abbé Martin [sic],[4] in which she realizes he was "an imposter whom for years I had taken as a representative of God on earth," which makes her wonder if "perhaps God was stupid!"[5] Abbé Martin provides a model for the fictional Abbé Mirande, in which the protagonist Marguerite realizes one day, during confession, that the abbé she had regarded as a direct emissary of god was no more than a prying gossip, and is aghast she had confused him with God. Compare the fictional description to Beauvoir's autobiographical one, of a God "so ridiculous that soon I began to doubt his existence … in the midst of a great silence it appeared to me the world had suddenly grown empty."[6] In the short story, after her "epiphany," Marguerite explores the life previously forbidden to her – including night life. She reflects upon the jazz bar:

> I went there once as I had gone to Mass, with the same ardour, and I had scarcely changed my God – the jazz moved me as deeply as the great voice of the organ in earlier days. Ever since Denis had told me that piece about sin being the space yawning wide for God, vice had given me the same ecstatic

---

2 Beauvoir, *When Things of the Spirit Come First*, 15.
3 Beauvoir, *When Things of the Spirit*, 170.
4 Beauvoir, *Memoirs of a Dutiful Daughter*, 134.
5 Beauvoir, *Memoirs of a Dutiful Daughter*, 134.
6 Beauvoir, *When Things of the Spirit Come First*, 172.

feeling I had felt as a child before the real presence of the Holy Sacrament ...
In my own way, I too was serving the things of the spirit.[7]

This frank fictional account of the conversion of a pious bourgeois girl into an existential free spirit, repeated in the first volume of Beauvoir's autobiography, gives a prescient assessment of the function of those things she used to ascribe to "religion:" Here, the "spirit" of the jazz club fills a "yawning" space, and provides "a great silence," with "things of the spirit," movements that will continue to operate within her long after her rejection of the Catholic tradition.

In *Memoirs of a Dutiful Daughter*, where Beauvoir details her pious upbringing by her ultra-orthodox Catholic mother and atheist father, she assumes that her audience understands the demands of Catholic piety, and focuses instead on her private reflections on God and her relationship with Him. She only mentions in passing the requirement that she say prayers daily and attend Mass frequently, as well as referring to her experiments with what she calls mysticism and her own readings of the *Lives of the Saints*, the Gospels, and the Mystics. In short, she had a childhood saturated in both the literary and ritual traditions of French Catholicism. As she recalls much later in *All Said and Done*, "My religious instruction was in fact very thorough: as for the Gospels, I knew long passages by heart."[8] Describing the ardor of her piety as a child, Beauvoir writes of God, "I loved him with all the passion I brought to life itself ... I ardently desired to grow closer to God, but I didn't know how to go about it."[9] Increasingly, her love of this earthly paradise becomes identified with the God she loved so much:

> One day something inside me would find itself in harmony with the scent of the honeysuckle ... From dawn to dusk there hummed over the unchanging plains a life that was everlastingly renewed. In the face of the changing sky, constancy was seen to be something more than routine habit, and growing up did not necessarily mean denying one's true self.[10]

This leads her to the discovery that "the harder I pressed myself against the earth, the closer I got to him, and every country act was an act of adoration."[11] At the same time, she reveals that "it seemed to me that

---

7 Beauvoir, *When Things of the Spirit Come First*, 182.
8 Beauvoir, *All Said and Done*, 459.
9 Beauvoir, *Memoirs of a Dutiful Daughter*, 74.
10 Beauvoir, *Memoirs of a Dutiful Daughter*, 125.
11 Beauvoir, *Memoirs of a Dutiful Daughter*, 125.

He needed my eyes in order that the trees might have their colours,"[12] suggesting that she understands her relationship to the Divine as one of reciprocity, a theme that will reemerge in her existential philosophy. This suggests that the function of her beloved creator is integrated both with her physical adoration of the earth itself, and with her belief in her own primacy as the object of divine affection. A paradoxical reciprocity ensues: the desired Creator is found by the ecstatic child in His very own Creation, the creation she loves as much as Him, and to Him, she remains the adorer whom He loves as much as his creation. Here, she also echoes the kind of relationship she analyses later in her chapter "The Mystic" in *The Second Sex*. There, she observes "human love and divine love melt into one another not because the latter is a sublimation of the former but because the former is also a movement toward transcendence."[13] This is a generous admission regarding the attraction of "mysticism" in a chapter that otherwise mocks its subjects for their unconscious obedience to sexist expectation. As she notes immediately thereafter, "the woman in love has to save her contingent existence by uniting with the Whole, incarnated in a sovereign Person."[14] In this quotation, she dryly satirizes the inconsistency of that which is expected of woman by Catholic "religion" – to join an infinite absolute absolutely when, as the philosopher has argued, we are finite contingencies. Satire aside, clearly Beauvoir accepts this aporia, an aporia that is itself the articulation of the mystery that intrigues Beauvoir throughout her writing life.

Certeau's formulation of the mystic explicates this mystery in a manner consistent with Beauvoir: "'May I not be separated from thee.' *Nichte Ohne*. Not without thee,"[15] a phrase that suggests "One sole being is lacking, and all is lacking."[16] Beauvoir's insight into the "mystic" aporia – of the contingent being longing for the impossible absolute – will find its resolution in her existential ethic. It may be that the "mystic" awareness witnessed here is located in her own grasp of ambiguity – that for every insistence upon our freedom and moral autonomy, there is the check of the necessary entanglement with others. These others, although we are told each must strive to preserve our freedom as they strive to preserve their own, are the limit of our situation and thus constitute a boundary that contradicts our ontological freedom. It may be that Beauvoir flees religion only to reinvest

---

12 Beauvoir, *Memoirs of a Dutiful Daughter*, 125.
13 Beauvoir, *The Second Sex*, 709.
14 Beauvoir, *The Second Sex*, 709.
15 Certeau, *The Mystic Fable*, 2.
16 Certeau, *The Mystic Fable*, 2.

its mechanisms in her ethics of the appeal and promise, consciously rejecting the absolute while repeatedly seeking to regain it, something of which she is very aware. This movement is reminiscent of Simone Weil's "purifying atheism," losing God to find God again.[17] The fact of her awareness of her attraction to the absolute, contradictory as it is, is perhaps at the same time the admission that she continues to accept in some way the possibility of metaphysical transcendence, at least as an "undecidable."

As she grows up, she "began to reject a dry-as-dust morality in favour of a more lively mysticism."[18] Although this "mysticism" is again not defined, only implied, it seems to include unspecified experiments in mortifications of her flesh and a vicarious reveling in the "mystical" accounts of the saints. However, she admits that when she had performed these experiments, she,

> never had the impression I was growing any closer to God. I longed for apparitions, ecstasies; I yearned for something to happen inside or outside me; but nothing came, and in the end my spiritual exercises were more and more like make believe.[19]

As she begins to experience questions of doubt regarding church teaching, she is drawn more and more to intense experiences of sublime beauty and overwhelming dissolution into an Other, one she identifies at first with her God. Nevertheless, her joyous, embodied communion with nature led her to eventually conclude, in an inversion of Pascal's wager, that she would prefer to love this beautiful earth now, rather than forgo it for a heaven that may not be. Inevitably, one evening at the family summer home at Meyrignac,

> I dipped my hands into the cherry laurel leaves. I listened to the gurgling of the water, and I knew then that nothing would make me give up my earthly joys. 'I no longer believe in God,' I told myself, with no great surprise. That was proof: if I had believed in him, I should not have allowed myself to offend him so light-heartedly. I had always thought that the world was a small price to pay for eternity; but it was worth more than that, because I loved the world, and it was suddenly God whose price was small: from now on, his name would have to be a cover for nothing more than a mirage ...

---

17 As cited previously in Baring's discussion of Weil's influence on Derrida. See Baring, *The Young Derrida*, 63.
18 Beauvoir, *Memoirs of a Dutiful Daughter*, 134.
19 Beauvoir, *Memoirs of a Dutiful Daughter*, 134.

That is why I felt so little surprise when I became aware of his absence in heaven and in my heart.[20]

Concluding that "god was no longer relevant to me," she nevertheless acknowledges throughout her long writing career her persistent attraction toward an impossible absolute, and recurring encounters of joyous communion with the beauties of the earth. However, these encounters are evanescent, and her longing for a union with an unknown Other persists. After her conversion away from theism and piety and into atheism, she describes how, to soothe the turmoils of adolescence,

> I entered into exalted trances, as on those evenings that I used to gaze upon the sky full of moving clouds behind the distant blue of the hills. I was both the landscape and its beholder: I existed only through myself, and for myself. I was grateful for an exile that had driven me to find such lonely and such lofty joys ...[21]

Such a passage testifies to the play of religion as response: Beauvoir initially and unconsciously responds to the Catholic tradition in faith, promising to believe in that holy narrative and to keep its teachings safe and sound. Eventually concluding that "God" was not a relevant category of thought, she nevertheless continues to respond to the appeal of the "earthly joys" that she yearns to make identical to herself. Similarly to Derrida's proposal for a "god of the interior," she seems to have discovered early on the mechanism for meaning-making lies within, and between oneself and others. In a lengthy reflection on the "disquiet" she and her contemporaries experienced during their adolescence, drawn to "immoralism," she notes,

> So immoralism was not a just a snook cocked at society; it was a way of reaching God. Believers and unbelievers alike used this name. According to some, it signified an inaccessible presence, and to others, a vertiginous absence, and I had no trouble amalgamating Claudel and Gide; in both of them, God was defined, in relation to the bourgeois world, as the *other*, and everything that was other was a manifestation of something divine.[22]

This reconstruction of her responses to the ethical fashion of her youth shows how early on, the connection is made between the divine object

---

20 Beauvoir, *Memoirs of a Dutiful Daughter*, 137.
21 Beauvoir, *Memoirs of a Dutiful Daughter*, 191.
22 Beauvoir, *Memoirs of a Dutiful Daughter*, 196.

of desire and otherness. Moreover, the site of that otherness is multiple – here "God," there the beauty of the earth, or the gaze of the beloved person. It looks forward to her more mature reflections on where to destine one's desire, and thus where to find meaning: "everything that was other was a manifestation of something divine," a formula that anticipates the other as locus of meaning, founded in the act of faith.

Struggling to locate herself and her "lofty" longings in her post-Roman Catholic condition, she briefly considers, under the influence of Plotinus and her friend Merleau-Ponty, "cultivating a mystical theology." She asks "why shouldn't a mystical theology be possible? 'I want to touch God or become God' I declared in my journal. All through that year I abandoned myself intermittently to these deliriums."[23] Still attracted to the ecstatic reveries afforded to her by the earth, she describes how, while at La Grillière, the family's country estate, to prepare for her *agrégation*,

> In those woods and meadows undisturbed by man, I thought I touched that superhuman reality I aspired to. I knelt down to pick a flower and suddenly I felt riveted to the earth, with all the weight of heavens on my shoulders; I couldn't move: it was both an agony and an ecstasy which brought eternity within my grasp. I returned to Paris convinced that I had passed through a mystical experience, and attempted to bring it on again. I had read St. John of the Cross: 'In order to go the way thou knowest not, thou must go the way thou knowest not.' Reversing this phrase, I saw in the obscurity of my ways a sign that I was moving toward fulfilment. I would descend into the very depths of my being, and rise toward the zenith in which I embraced the Whole .... it was tempting to let myself believe that I had attained the Unknown. I cultivated these states with the utmost complacency.[24]

Here, the "mystical" practice is directed at achieving a transcendent state, one that is "superhuman," eternal and obscure, in which she could grasp the "Whole" and attain the "Unknown." The theme of this passage is that of transcendence, transcendence understood as that experience which exceeds quotidian experience and rationality. She shares these mystical experiences with "Pradelle" – her pseudonym for her close friend Maurice Merleau-Ponty – who retorts that he finds it "not of the slightest interest." Thereafter, she "did not try to bring them on again."[25] Eventually, perhaps chastened by his remark, she determined never to call upon god again,[26]

---

23   Beauvoir, *Memoirs of a Dutiful Daughter*, 261.
24   Beauvoir, *Memoirs of a Dutiful Daughter*, 267.
25   Beauvoir, *Memoirs of a Dutiful Daughter*.
26   Beauvoir, *Memoirs of a Dutiful Daughter*, 272.

replacing her former piety with a passion for literature. As Lecarme-Tabone observes, "L'écriture, pourtant, se substitue bien, en fait, à la foi religieuse ..."²⁷ [Writing, however, is a good substitute for religious faith].

This attraction to the Absolute Other and longing for mystic union with something is never entirely absent from her various texts and finds another site in her passion for writing, where she can experience another kind of transcendence. In *The Prime of Life*, which recounts her early career as a teacher and her relationship with Sartre, she describes the two of them as "a couple of mystics. Sartre had an unqualified faith in Beauty, which he treated as inseparable from Art, while I attached supreme importance to Life."²⁸ This passage suggests that she is using "mystic" as a term for the ideal and evanescent object of one's longing: a case of "beauty" for Sartre, and of "Life" for herself. She qualifies this somewhat when recalling her reflections on her vocation as a writer:

> I had rejected the notion of divinity but not all aspects of the supernatural. Obviously I knew that a work wrought on earth can only communicate in earthly terms. But there were some that seemed to me to have broken free from their creator and absorbed something of the meaning he had tried to put into them. There they stood, four-square and independent, dumb, inscrutable, like huge abandoned totems: in them alone I made contact with some vital absolute element. It may seem paradoxical that I, who was so much in love with life, should have continued to demand this inhuman purity from art. But there was a logic in my obstinacy: since art led me away from life, it could attain fulfilment only by denying life's claims.²⁹

She suggests here that the facticity of a work of art, here writing, in its utter independence from its author, produces a transcendent scene of meaning – transcendent in that it exists apart from its creator, independent and yet accessible. This transcendent quality in her creations fulfills the same function for Beauvoir's narrators as "god" did previously, providing a condition that "denied life's claims," such as finitude, while providing "contact with some vital absolute element." She later makes this connection more explicit, when describing her struggle to write *America Day by Day*, "...it did not give me what I had always demanded of writing up till then: the feeling of risking and the same time transcending myself, an almost religious

---

27 Lecarme-Tabone, "Introduction." *Mémoires d'une jeune fille rangée de Simone de Beauvoir*, 85.
28 Beauvoir, *The Prime of Life*, 26.
29 Beauvoir, *The Prime of Life*, 38.

joy"[30] Here she unites the risk and transcendence afforded in writing with the "religious," a term that she seems to associate with a "superhuman reality" she aspired to. By this account, the joy she had experienced in writing, though evanescent, has now replaced her earlier encounters with the joy of ecstatic piety. As she narrates how her relationship with Sartre matured, and required her to establish her own place within it more precisely, she admits

> the notion of salvation had lingered in my mind after belief in God had vanished, and my chief conviction was that each individual was responsible for securing his own. The difficulty nagging at me was not so much a social as a moral, almost a religious, contradiction in terms.[31]

Although her world was now entirely earthbound and human, she nevertheless continues to think in the language of her Catholic girlhood, translating its concepts, like "salvation" and "religious joy," into her existential context. Above all, she continues to long for Being:

> If I drank a little too much one evening I was liable to burst into floods of tears, and my hankering after the Absolute would be aroused again. Once more I became aware of the vanity of human endeavour and the imminence of death; I would reproach Sartre for allowing himself to be duped by the hateful mystification known as "life."[32]

The crushing awareness of her own mortality and finitude is made more acute after her rejection of God, yet she experiences the paradox of longing more than ever for that absolute state of "Being" that her developing existential consciousness rejects as impossible. She was, as they say, still trapped in the metaphysical enclosure without even the consolation of recognizing this fact. Her tendency toward abstract positions when the war broke out testifies to this. As she puts it, up until the end of the Phony war,

> our life, like that of all petites bourgeois intellectuals, was in fact mainly characterized by its lack of reality ... Nor could I break free from my universalist abstractions; I remained riddled with bourgeois idealism and aestheticism. Above all, my emotionally ambivalent obsession with happiness blinded me to political realities.[33]

---

30 Beauvoir, *After the War: Hard Times*, 127.
31 Beauvoir, *The Prime of Life*, 54.
32 Beauvoir, *The Prime of Life*, 167.
33 Beauvoir, *The Prime of Life*, 288.

This reflection, one of several, frankly acknowledges her ongoing attraction to "universalist abstractions" and "idealism," as a part of her residual bourgeois worldview, one that war will disrupt and cause her to critique.

At the same time, she also treasures the ritual of gathering friends and comrades for all night revelry, which she calls "*fêtes*." In one of several accounts she has given about the power of the *fête*, she observes:

> if hope is rekindled in the very midst of despair, if you regain your hold upon the world and the times – then the magic moment catches fire and you can plunge into it and be consumed with it: that is a "*fête*." The distant horizon is uncertain still, half threatening, half promising: that is why every *fête* has a quality of pathos about it.[34]

This assessment of the authentic *fête* possesses the same qualities as her other mystic experiences: non-rational, intense, all-encompassing, and evanescent. Perhaps most strikingly, the horizon viewed through the *fête* – "Uncertain still, half threatening, half promising," recalls Derrida's description of the space of faith in "Faith and Knowledge," the desert within the desert, receding from what it reveals, one of the sources of that originary faith that proceeds from an invincible hope for justice. Beauvoir may have entered the war with a life characterized by its "lack of reality," but her experiences of her own privations – separated from Sartre during his internment as a prisoner of war, rationing, blackouts, lockdowns, and the jarring injustices she witnessed – especially the disappearances of Jewish friends – gave birth to her political consciousness, and to her acute sense of existential situatedness. Describing herself in August of 1944 as "*dépaysée*," in a radically transformed world, she recalls how she nevertheless

> contemplated the future with some confidence. History was not my enemy since, in the last resort, my hopes had been fulfilled. Indeed, it has bestowed on me the most poignant joy I had ever experienced.[35]

This "poignant joy" was her experience of the liberation of Paris, a moment of communion she vividly describes in *The Prime of Life*, and which was the fulfillment of the promise offered by those *fêtes* she enjoyed. She recalls how in the aftermath of the war, she thought how,

---

34 Beauvoir, *The Prime of Life*, 453.
35 Beauvoir, *The Prime of Life*, 473.

> To act in concert with all men, to struggle, to accept death if need be, that life might keep its meaning – by holding fast to these precepts, I felt, I would master that darkness when human lamentation arose. Or would I?[36]

Awakened to her solidarity with every other person, through the particularity of each one's suffering and joy, she nevertheless is sensitive to the persistent ambiguity of the human situation, "half threatening, half promising," and at the same time, the only source of meaning.

In the final volume of her autobiography, 1972's *All Said and Done*, she reflects in retrospect:

> Like all individuals, I sought to overtake my being and merge with it; and in order to do so I based myself upon those experiences in which I had the illusion of having achieved this. Knowing meant directing my awareness toward the world, as did all the meditation of my childhood, withdrawing the world from the void of the past and from the darkness of absence: when I lost myself in the object upon which I gazed, or in moments of physical or emotional ecstasy, or in the delight of memory, or in the heart-raising anticipation of what was to come, it seemed to me I brought about the impossible junction between the in-itself and the for-itself. And I also wanted to realize myself in books that, like those I had loved, would be existing objects for others, but objects haunted by a presence, my presence.[37]

The recurring themes: resisting absence, losing oneself in ecstasy, impossible paradoxical union of otherness, the quest for transcendence, usually identified as "happiness," it is all here at the latter half of this life, as it was in the beginning. At the same time, with a fitting ambiguity, she became and remained an existential atheist, one who deemed the Catholic religion as a case of "merely reproducing a form of behaviour that was inculcated by their upbringing and that is observed in their circle,"[38] and justified by psychologically self-serving "humbug."[39] In this observation, she instantiates the scene of religion as the drive to gather and bind, in this case bourgeois society, into a self-perpetuating totality, even as she asserts the impossibility of such a totality in the contingent multivalent world.

As the evidence suggests, a significant element in Beauvoir's Catholic and atheist reflections is her attraction to and engagement with what she calls mysticism. Beauvoir explicitly concerned herself with mystic

---

36 Beauvoir, *The Prime of Life*, 473.
37 Beauvoir, *All Said and Done*, 29.
38 Beauvoir, *All Said and Done*, 460.
39 Beauvoir, *All Said and Done*, 462.

tradition, as a reader of the mystic saints in her youth, and as a critic. Reprising the passage from "The Mystic" in *The Second Sex*:

> Love has been assigned to woman as her supreme vocation, and when she addresses it to man, she is seeking God in him: if circumstances deny her human love, she will choose to worship the divinity in God himself ... The Beloved is always more or less absent; he communicates with her, his worshipper, in ambiguous signs; she only knows his heart by an act of faith; and the more superior to her he seems, the more impenetrable his behaviour seems to her.[40]

This account of contemporary "woman" as a figure of "mysticism," opens this chapter in *The Second Sex*, followed by a phenomenological description of the mystic calling, in which she establishes the ambiguous play of desire for the Other that drives the mystic discourse. In this description, Beauvoir foreshadows observations by Certeau in *The Mystic Fable*. Both discourse about the post-medieval Christian mystics of the 16th and 17th centuries; both observe the performance of the erotic and the gendered in the "lives of the saints." Both focus on the mystic performance as a resistance to the institutional hegemony of the time, although Beauvoir restricts her approbation to Teresa of Avila and John of the Cross, disdaining others, like Madame Guyon as confusing "mysticism with erotomania."[41] More importantly, both Beauvoir and Certeau read the substitution of the One for another one: in Beauvoir, God as the Beloved One is substituted with situated man, a movement that harmonizes with the contention that the mechanisms of the scene of religion are reproduced, in this case, in gender relations of the early 20th century.

Certeau's observes that the mystics emerge from social conditions of decline: impoverished nobility, dispossessed gentry caught in the great upheavals driving these societies toward the "secular," a secular that engenders a new eroticism. A practical consequence of this is that it provides an opening for women – traditionally identified as carnal, material, and emotional – in the otherwise masculine ecclesia. Let us also recall that Certeau argues,

> This was no mere coincidence. Both sprang from a "nostalgia" connected with the progressive decline of God as One, as object of love. Both are equally the effects of separation.[42]

---

40 Beauvoir, *The Second Sex*, 709.
41 Beauvoir, *The Second Sex*, 711.
42 Certeau, *The Mystic Fable*, 4.

Beauvoir understands these "effects of separation" and lives in circumstances, as a woman, as one disaffected from the tradition, that repeats the mystic scene. Like many of the mystic writers of the 16th and 17th century, Beauvoir is born into conditions of social decline: a dispossessed branch of an affluent French petit bourgeois family, a pious and obedient Roman Catholic mother, and a disaffected atheist father. Like many of her mystic antecedents, she experiences a longing for the transcendent absolute One that consumes her even as she becomes increasingly distrustful of the Church's requirements for the faithful. In this, born a woman, to an aristocratic family in declining circumstances, in a time of social, political and economic chaos, Beauvoir's material circumstances are remarkably close to Certeau's description of the late Renaissance mystics. Whether or not these circumstances are definitive, it is possible to see the ways in which they provide the context for her rejection of her institutions and explorations of alternatives.

As Beauvoir begins to contest and resist the "serious" tradition she is presented with, she also suffers from a "nostalgia" that sees the site of the One change locations, from the divine to the human. And yet, she is careful to distinguish between what she calls "erotomania" and a worthy project for one's freedom. She notes in this chapter, for the first time defining "mysticism," that the woman given over to the mystic is "groping for the supreme source of values. That is what every mystic is aiming for."[43] She rejects the argument that "the poverty of language makes it necessary for the mystic to borrow this erotic vocabulary"[44] because it truncates the unity of the existent individual:

> she also has only one body, and she borrows from earthly love not only words but also physical attitudes; she has the same behavior when offering herself to God as offering herself to man.[45]

However, for Beauvoir this does not diminish the validity of her feelings, nor does it compromise the integrity of the mystic experience. Beauvoir, consistent in her view of the human being, insists that the subject *is* the body, and can therefore only destine her actions through her body, in this case, the action of seeking union with the source of all values. Citing Teresa of Avila, she observes that "bodily gestures can be part of the expression

---

43 Beauvoir, *The Second Sex*, 711.
44 Beauvoir, *The Second Sex*, 712.
45 Beauvoir, *The Second Sex*, 712.

of freedom"[46] when they act toward the object of desire, the object that arouses desire in the subject:

> Thus, in one movement, Saint Teresa seeks to unite with God and experience this union in her body; she is not slave to her nerves and hormones; rather, she should be admired for the intensity of a faith that penetrates to the most intimate regions of her flesh. In truth, as Saint Teresa understood, the value of a mystical experience is measured not by how it has been subjectively experienced but by its objective scope.[47]

Teresa is valorized by Beauvoir because in seeking the supreme source of values, she "situates the dramatic problem of the relationship between the individual and the transcendent Being in a highly intellectual way,"[48] in which her experience far exceeded the boundaries of conventional sexuality. However, Teresa, like John of the Cross, is for Beauvoir "the striking exception:" others, like Mme Guyon and Angela de Foligno, are aiming for "the redemption of their femininity"[49] rather than transcendence.[50]

Published in 1949, Beauvoir's observations on mysticism in *The Second Sex* anticipate many of the recent critical approaches to mysticism that have developed during the past 30 years. This chapter offers a fluid understanding that the object of desire is ambivalent – human here, divine there, and is in either case, "more or less absent." A testament to her own engagement with the primary mystical texts, she critiques the Christian mystic writers of the 16th and 17th centuries from the point of view of psychology, sociology, and in terms of gender. Her astute interpretation of mystic practice anticipates the recent political, psychological, feminist, and historiographical critiques of mysticism. Her insights look forward to recent feminist discourse on mysticism, which investigate the tradition of associating "the female" with "body/ecstatic/erotic/mysticism" and the historic evidence which challenges these associations.[51] The mystic discourse of women from the earliest evidence in the 5th century through the end of the 17th century is read as both a resistance to and a co-optation of the political and social boundaries prescribed for women from Tertullian through to Bernard of Clairvaux and the Inquisitors. The analyses of the

---

46 Beauvoir, *The Second Sex*, 712.
47 Beauvoir, *The Second Sex*, 713.
48 Beauvoir, *The Second Sex*, 713.
49 Beauvoir, *The Second Sex*, 713.
50 Beauvoir, *The Second Sex*, 713.
51 See Grace Janzen in *Power, Gender and Christian Mysticism*, Dyan Elliott in *The Bride of Christ Goes to Hell*, and Amy Hollywood's *Sensible Ecstasy*.

"mystical" discourses observe the ambiguity with which one can read the erotically charged language of many of the "saints." Some instances suggest a thinly veiled substitution for carnal sexuality, whereas in other instances it indicates the only satisfactory metaphor to describe the transcendent, all-encompassing experience of divine love.

Beauvoir's distinction between "erotomania" and the quest for the supreme source of values also anticipates Certeau's psychological history of the rise and persecution of the "mystics" that culminated in the trials at Loudun. Certeau examines the psychological affects of the decline of central institutional authority and rise of discrete "movements." In his examination of Jeanne des Anges, one of the "possessed" at Loudon who later toured France exhibiting "divine" tattoos on her hands, he observes that it becomes apparent in reading her own testimony that she authored a troubling relationship of manipulation and abuse in the name of propping up a divine mystery.[52] However, like Beauvoir, Certeau does not insist on reducing all mystic discourse to its sometimes troubling provenance, but seeks to understand that for some, it is an endless quest for One who is absent.

As we have seen, Beauvoir describes herself as having a "mystical aptitude." She attests several times to having passed through a "mystical" experience in communing with the natural world, and does not forsake the exhortations of those mystics she admired. She rarely defines "mysticism," but we may infer that she understands it as the fulfillment of the desire for union with the transcendent, a union that engages the whole individual and which exceeds rational expression. She puts this most bluntly when she says: "I had rejected the notion of divinity but not all aspects of the supernatural,"[53] a sentiment also echoed by her character Marcelle, who says ruefully, "she wishes she still believed in God so that she could go and cry in a church as she had done when she was a child: human things left her deeply unsatisfied."[54] Rejecting divinity but "not the supernatural" confirms her persistent openness to experiences that transcend quotidian expectation. However, this "openness" is also a void, an absence that she longs to fill, impossibly, with "being." In *After the War*, she recalls "God had died when I was fourteen; nothing had replaced him: the absolute only existed in the negative, like a horizon forever lost to view."[55] This is the heart of her understanding of ambiguity – a longing to be, a seeking to

---

52  Certeau, *The Possession at Loudun*, 162.
53  Beauvoir, *The Prime of Life*, 38.
54  Beauvoir, *When Things of the Spirit Come First*, 24.
55  Beauvoir, *After the War*, 46.

be one with an other absolute "being," at the same time acknowledging that "Being" is an illusion, "lost from view," and so an impossible object of desire. This also draws near to Certeau's scene of the mystic, a scene he infers we still inhabit, a "region we cannot identify, as if we had been stricken by the separation long before realizing it. When this situation finds expression, it may still borrow the words of the ancient Christian prayer: 'May I not be separated from Thee.'"[56] The persistent longing for the absent remains a powerful trope in her texts, an acknowledgement of the "negative" that had once lit up the horizon of her desire, but is now "forever lost to view." And yet, it still hovers on the other side of her imagination, a work of mourning that is always in progress.

It is Beauvoir's suspicion toward and rejection of presence, of a static, eternal Being, and all the implications of such stasis, that led her to Existentialism, and to her "Ethics of Ambiguity." Her argument for rejecting traditional metaphysics – the metaphysics of an absolute eternal unchanging "heaven of Ideas" and "God," – is both experiential and logical. The experience of realizing god was no longer relevant to her life is witnessed in her *Memoirs*; the logical implications of belief in an all encompassing totality are taken up in *Pyrrhus and Cineas*, where she argues that the very concept of an eternal absolute to unite with and be encompassed by leaves no room for movement, a space where "all figures disappear," and "presence cannot be distinguished from absolute absence."[57] The last observation establishes a logically incompatible paradox that she addresses with her program in *The Ethics of Ambiguity*, where she affirms the human ontological truth that we are free. There is no external source of value or meaning except that which we make and that the meaning we create requires our relationship to others, while, paradoxically, transcendence is found in the movement of our projects, projects "that concern others, [as] they concern me."

Beauvoir's autobiographies also detail how her rejection of Roman Catholic piety emerges in step with her descriptions of a bewildering erotic maturation, echoing Certeau's account of the trajectory of the mystic tradition wherein, as we have noted, the demythified divine is displaced by the mythification of love.[58] While this movement is true in Beauvoir's *Memoirs of a Dutiful Daughter*, her philosophical texts and novels reveal a

---

56 Certeau, *The Mystic Fable*, 1.
57 Beauvoir, *Pyrrhus and Cineas*, 101.
58 Beauvoir, *The Prime of Life*, 54–57, details her deep confusion at her sexual longings, at her uncontrollable bodily urges in her early 20s, feelings matched only by her elevation of Sartre to "divine" status in her life.

nuanced understanding of the longing for that which is absent, for an absolute in an utterly secular world. She explicitly acknowledges this contradiction as one iteration of the heart of the human condition, which she defines as "ambiguity," a contradiction that she argues it is necessary to embrace, if one is to live an authentic human life.

As we have seen, out of her bourgeois French Catholic context, Beauvoir testifies to a persistent longing to unite "in-itself to the for-itself,"[59] or, in other words, her "self" with an "other." She treasures this longing for union with the absolute other, even as she admits its impossibility. The concept of an absolute is consistent with the traditional concept of "knowledge" – of those objects of thought that do not change, eternal and absolute. This knowledge is one of Derrida's two sources of religion, and a desire for it persists in Beauvoir, even after her "conversion" to existentialism. This may be explained in terms of Beauvoir's acceptance of the ubiquitous ambiguity of the human condition, which provides the conditions for the persistence of certain tropes of practice and existential understanding retained from her Roman Catholic rearing. She still seeks salvation, but now salvation means to be saved from the darkness of mortality and injustice. She still yearns for union with Being, knowing there is only becoming, and union with a transcendence that contradicts the contingency of existence. What of the second source of religion, the originary faith that founds all promises, all hope, the faith valorized in Derrida's analysis? Her faith, once directed at the absent deity of the Catholic tradition, the absolute Other named "God," is now aimed at the human person in the I-Other binary, the binary which she claims is the foundation of meaning. The next chapter will examine the role of the Other in her *Ethics of Ambiguity*, and the originary faith it entails.

---

59  Beauvoir, *All Said and Done*, 29.

## Chapter 4

## The Other Shore

As we have seen, Beauvoir dismisses the Roman Catholic rite, as well as faith in God, metaphysics or any external powers. Instead, in her philosophy, she reassigns faith in its iteration, according to Derrida, of that originary promise between each other. She offers such faith to the appeal of human relationships, and the promise that these relationships offer for justifying our lives. I want to show how the faith that is implicit in Beauvoir's ethics functions in the same way as the "originary faith" we have examined in Derrida's analysis of religion, the faith that arises out of that desire for justice which alone allows for the hope of that "universalizable culture of singularities." he insists is the context for justice in "Faith and Knowledge." This faith is implicated in that longing for an absolute other, a longing which ironically arrives at Beauvoir's insistence on the human source of any meaning, in which she affirms that the only viable "absolute" is the "other," that other who can return the gaze by which I know I exist.

Beauvoir's ethic is situated squarely in the inescapable and necessary fact of human relationships. Beauvoir scholars[1] have examined the theme

---

[1] Deutscher, "Enemies and Reciprocities," 656–71.
 A putative deconstruction of the inflections of the "other" in *The Second Sex*, *Pyrrhus and Cineas*, and less so, *The Ethics of Ambiguity*. Deutscher's careful reading reveals the scope and limits of how the other is constructed – interestingly, gender is not one of its categories.
 Tidd, "The Self-Other Relation in Beauvoir's Ethics and Autobiography," 168–74. Tidd argues that the ethics constituted by the relation to the other enjoined in Beauvoir's philosophy in the 40s is performed throughout her many autobiographical texts.

of the "other" as it reflects Beauvoir's engagement with the philosophical tradition, especially Hegel. One can read Beauvoir's oeuvre as "as a sustained meditation on the problem of the other's consciousness,"[2] following Beauvoir's self-assessment that the problem she engaged with throughout her career was that of the problem of the "the consciousness of the other."[3] This can be seen in Beauvoir's lifelong engagement with Hegel's *Phenomenology of Spirit*. Reviewing the mutlivalent possibilities for interpreting Hegel's dialectic of consciousness, O'Brien suggests:

> Hegel is not imposing his account of the dialectic upon the history of consciousness in his writings, as is often considered to be the case, but rather he is bearing witness to its workings. It is not used in order to make evident the movement of consciousness toward recognition but rather the dialectic is evidenced or revealed through his description of this history. This is a phenomenology. That is, the dialectic was not his methodological presupposition but rather was his philosophical discovery. This is a subtle yet significant difference ...[4]

While Beauvoir finds an inspired template for thinking about the problem of the Other in Hegel's text, "what Beauvoir seeks to do in and through her readings of the *Phenomenology* is to extract the history of consciousness from its metaphysical groundings and replant it within the framework of her version of existentialism."[5] It follows then, that for Beauvoir, the crux of Hegel's dialectic of self-consciousness – "recognition" – not only provides the conditions for the self but also provides the conditions for the relationship with the Other, the other who only in her freedom can confer meaning on our existence, by giving a future to our projects through the content of the appeal to which the other responds. Where Hegel fails for Beauvoir is in his insistence on the totalizing essence that is the appearances. She overcomes the problem of assuming an ontological totality by relocating the human being in the existential context.

Beauvoir reads the response of the other to one's project as a pledge – a pledge to honor the other's project and, out of one's freedom, adopt it. Drawing near to Derrida's "originary faith," this response, this pledge,

---

O'Brien, *Simone de Beauvoir and The Problem of The Other's Consciousness*. O'Brien argues for a sustained preoccupation with the "problem of the other," mediated through her engagement with Hegel, throughout Beauvoir's works.

2   O'Brien, *Simone de Beauvoir and The Problem of The Other's Consciousness*, 2.
3   O'Brien, *Simone de Beauvoir and The Problem of The Other's Consciousness*, 1.
4   O'Brien, *Simone de Beauvoir and The Problem of The Other's Consciousness*, 6.
5   O'Brien, *Simone de Beauvoir and The Problem of The Other's Consciousness*, 21.

gives meaning to one's existence by transforming one's end into a new departure for the other who honors this project. The faith at issue is located in this possibility – a contingent possibility, as not every project of an other will be honored, nor will every other honor ours. She insists we must be faced with morally free men: each individual must freely choose those others who are imicable – in love and friendship or even necessity – sometimes in antinomonies of ethical dilemmas. Every project involves risk – the risk of failure – but the will to pursue it also exhibits this faith, the same faith that finds its justification in the response to the appeal of the project. This implicit faith, this *rapport* that is established between individuals binds them, not to an impossible knowledge but, instead, to each other's projects. Founded in an originary faith that arises from the "messianicity without messianism" that is making its way "through the risks of absolute night," Beauvoir's account of this rapport performs that faith which Derrida suggests is the only hope for the justice particular to our post-enlightenment singular bonded selves.[6]

As Beauvoir is engaged in a "sustained meditation on the other's consciousness," it is her engagement with Hegel, which began in the summer of 1940, that allows her to define the problem and its implications with philosophical clarity. This focus also supports the contention that Beauvoir is, by intellectual choice and situation, thinking her Enlightenment inheritance, particularly the inheritance of autonomous self, the self whom Derrida reads as corresponding to the the machinery of the religious. A review of her writing during the 1940s allows me to present a genealogy of the Other in her thought, in which the Other, conceived first as "detached, absolute, unalterable, an alien conscience,"[7] is gradually understood to be the location of meaning and justification for one's existence. We can see this development in the three major texts of this period: *She Came to Stay, Pyrrhus and Cineas*, and *The Ethics of Ambiguity*. Although some recent scholarship has reviewed the development of Beauvoir's thought in both her fiction and philosophy during this period,[8] no one has reviewed it for the purpose of explicating the role of the other as it functions in the scene of religion, which I propose here.

Beauvoir's first attempt at fiction, the long unpublished *When Things of the Spirit Come First*, reflects her preoccupation at that time with critiquing

---

6   Derrida, "Faith and Knowledge," 56.
7   Beauvoir, *She Came to Stay*, 292.
8   Specifically, O'Brien's unpublished thesis, *Simone de Beauvoir and The Problem of The Other's Consciousness*; and Scholz and Musset, *The Contradictions of Freedom*.

the "serious" pose of bourgeois society. In five loosely connected stories, she describes the effects of bad faith propositions upon individuals, and the existential consequences of rejecting it. By contrast, her next novel, *She Came to Stay*, written between 1938 and 1941, begins with a character who, ostensibly free from the shackles of bourgeois seriousness, nevertheless must discover the Other, and the existential ramifications of this. Françoise, the protagonist of *She Came to Stay*, is acutely aware of herself as a conscious being, freely engaging with a world that, in her estimation, ontologically requires her own eyes and mind to exist. She lives a full and well organized life in a contingent relationship with Pierre, the love of her life, until Xavière enters their world. In the course of mutely watching Pierre become emotionally entangled with Xavière, Françoise discovers the "other" who cannot be sublated to her own consciousness, and who persistently challenges and disrupts Françoise's understanding and desires.

This text follows the trajectory of Hegel's dialectic of self-discovery in *Phenomenology of Spirit*. Françoise is first presented as one totally oblivious to the possibilities of consciousness outside her own. Indeed, she embodies a breathtaking solipsism:

> When she was not there, the smell of dust, the half-light and their forlorn solitude did not exist for anyone; they did not exist at all. And now she was not there. The red of the carpet gleamed through the darkness like a timid nightlight. He exercised that power: her presence snatched things from their unconsciousness; she gave them their colour, their smell ... She alone evoked the significance of these abandoned places, of these slumbering things. She was there and they belonged to her. The world belonged to her.[9]

Soon, however, with the arrival of Xavière, and the growing intimacy between Xavière and Pierre, Françoise's lover, she begins to perceive herself as indistinct and empty: "I am no one ... She did know with reasonable certainty what she was not: it was agonizing to know herself only as a series of negations."[10] This corresponds to the movement in Hegel's dialectic of the self coming to awareness of herself, of her own *ipseity*, as an object of thought, as something to be recognized. In Hegel,

> Self-consciousness is, first of all, simple *being-for-itself*, self-identical through the exclusion *from itself* of everything *other*; its essence and absolute object is,

---

9   Beauvoir, *She Came to Stay*, 1–2.
10  Beauvoir, *She Came to Stay*, 146.

for it, *the I*; and it is an individual in this immediacy, that is, in this *being of its being-for-itself*. Whatever is Other for it is an object characterized as unessential, with the character of the negative. But the *Other* is also self-consciousness; it emerges as an individual over against an individual.[11]

As Hegel cautions us, his dialectic of self-consciousness "has many sides and many meanings,"[12] but here we can read Françoise's experience as both one of self-recognition as well as one of Other-recognition. Françoise's self-perception is driven by her encounter with Xavière, so that Beauvoir offers us both her changing self-perception – as the *I*, as the *being-for-herself* – and at the same time, her perception of Xavière and her relationship with her as an other *being-for-herself*. Françoise sees Xavière mutilating her own flesh one night, and understands "behind that maniacal grin, was the threat of a danger more positive than any she had ever imagined. Something was there that hungrily hugged itself, that unquestionably existed on its own account."[13]

This threat echoes Hegel's claim that the activity of the other is a threat that must be negated:

> The relationship of both self-consciousnesses, therefore, is determined in such a way that they test themselves and each other in a life and death struggle. They must enter into this struggle because they must elevate their certainty of themselves, of *being-for-themselves*, into a truth with regard to themselves. And it is only through the risking of life that there is freedom ...[14]

However, following from Hegel's insistence on the double-movements inherent in this psychological process, at the same time that the self asserts itself against the Other, it simultaneously knows itself as an object to that Other, itself *as an other* to be negated. In this moment, wherein the self is aware of its dual positions, "it must be concerned with lifting the other independent essence, in order thereby to be certain of its own independent essence; secondly, this matter of lifting its [own] self because this other is itself."[15] In Hegel's next iteration of this dialectic, that of the Master and the Slave, the Master – the *being-for-itself*, and the Slave – the *being-for-another* – eventually recognize their mutual necessity: the Master

11  Hegel, *The Phenomenology of Spirit*, 1163.
12  Hegel, *The Phenomenology of Spirit*, 1162.
13  Beauvoir, *She Came to Stay*, 285.
14  Hegel, *The Phenomenology of Spirit*, 1163.
15  Hegel, *The Phenomenology of Spirit*, 1162.

as master requires the Slave to master; the Slave as slave, necessary to the master's identity, thus constitutes the Master, "lifting" the Slave to the level of the Master. In this "play of forces that constitutes self-consciousness," Hegel explains that,

> each is the middle for the other, through which each mediates itself with itself and merges with itself, and each is to itself and to the other an immediate Essence *being-for-itself*, which simultaneously is only *for itself* by virtue of this mediation. They recognize one another as mutually recognizing one another.[16]

Echoing Hegel's "play," Françoise's discovery of the total otherness of Xavière leads her to determine that the only solution to the threat she poses is to kill her, literally. Speaking with Pierre, Françoise protests the meaninglessness of abstractions (one of Beauvoir's persistent criticisms of Hegel) and explains that ideas have no value unless they "pass the test" of lived experience. Pierre offers:

> "The moment you acknowledge my conscience, you know that I acknowledge one in you too. That makes all the difference."
> "Perhaps," said Françoise. She stared in momentary perplexity at the bottom of her glass.
> "In short, that is friendship. Each renounces individual self-importance. But what if either refuses to renounce it?"
> "The friendship is impossible," said Pierre.[17]

Here is the crux of the problem that concerns Beauvoir with respect to Hegel's dialectic, the problem of the other as free to resist: to resist the implications of mediation, to resist friendship, to resist the particular relationship in its situation. Observing that "Xavière never renounced any part of herself," Françoise realizes, "One would have to kill Xavière."[18]

Beauvoir later reflects that this ending was not a satisfying or authentic solution to Françoise's problem,[19] inferring she is aware that the dialectic is left incomplete in her novel. She continues to explore this question of the Other, reframing it as the question of what is "our true relationship with other people."[20] During this period, she writes *Pyrrhus and Cineas* and

---

16  Hegel, *The Phenomenology of Spirit*, 1163.
17  Beauvoir, *She Came to Stay*, 303.
18  Beauvoir, *She Came to Stay*, 303.
19  Beauvoir, *The Prime of Life*, 479.
20  Beauvoir, *The Prime of Life*, 479.

*The Ethics of Ambiguity*, both of which take up the problem of the other and develop Hegel's notion of recognition into the foundation for an ethics and for ontological justification. Both of these texts will be examined here as they constitute the fullest articulation of Beauvoir's philosophy and are the evidence for her ethical performance in the play of the scene of religion.

In developing her theory of the "I-Other" binary as a locus for ethics, Beauvoir stages a subtle structure in her first published philosophical work, *Pyrrhus and Cineas*, and considers the question, why act? It anticipates, in a different context, the ethic that Beauvoir later develops more explicitly in *The Ethics of Ambiguity*. As Berghoffen has noted, "she will not take up the ethical question, how ought I to act? until she answers the existential question, Why act?"[21] In answering this question, Beauvoir argues that the defining quality of human existence is action, action that benefits from reflection when one's finite ends are accomplished. The title reflects this necessary ambiguity, as Pyrrhus argues for acting while Cineas evokes the power of reflection. Beauvoir's human being must act, because only in action do we live our constitutional transcendence, which is to ever succeed our given existence through the projects we imagine and manifest. To not act is to not live, but one's actions need to be toward something: they need to be destined.

The second theme in *Pyrrhus and Cineas* is, then, to what do I destine my actions so that they acquire meaning? The answer according, to Beauvoir, is other people – not God, not "humanity," not "infinity," or other tropes subject to indemnification, but other specific situated individuals. She argues that we act out our desired projects, and in this we appeal to other individuals who, responding to our project, take it up as their own, thereby validating the meaning of our project even as they freely appropriate it as their own. To act out our "projects," literally those projections of will into an unknown future out of an unstable present, involves risk: the risk of failure, the threat of opposition. However, Beauvoir also argues that it involves hope and promise, the promise of success, the hope of having our singular undertaking – irrevocably singular – taken up by an other. Implicit in her schema is the idea of faith: to act implies a faith that, despite the risk and the threat, an "other" will respond to the appeal of our project and so give it meaning beyond a solipsistic willing. In making this argument, Beauvoir transforms Hegel's figure of "recognition" as a kind of perpetual truce between hostile forces into a structure of mutually supporting and

---

21 Berghoffen's "Introduction" to Beauvoir, *Pyrrhus and Cineas*, 82.

beneficial human relations. Whereas in Hegel's scheme, consciousness of the other provokes a defensive response and a desire to sublate the perceived threat, at first by annihilation and, only secondly, as a necessary component of identity, Beauvoir moves directly from the second position – of recognizing the other as necessary to identity – and analyzes the implications of this recognition. She acknowledges the threat posed by the other but only as a threat of indifference toward or rejection of the appeal of one's project, and therefore the meaning afforded by the other's recognition. On the other hand, she also holds up the promise of response, of an other promising to take up one's project, one's appeal, as their own.

Beauvoir structures this essay strategically in order to make a compelling case for *ambiguity*, at first supporting the position of Pyrrhus who emphasizes that human beings are existents who *act*; then later, after anticipating and addressing the traditional and metaphysical objections to her argument, she will also affirm the stance of Cineas, that rest and reflection are also necessary. Interrogating Candide's exhortation to "cultivate your own garden," Beauvoir argues that we can only ever cultivate our own garden, as situated individuals who are nevertheless ontologically free. As individuals who are both subject and object, we found our relationship with the world in the choices we make. She claims "there exists no ready-made attachment between the world and me."[22] Rather,

> only that in which I recognize my being is mine, and I can only recognize it where it is engaged. In order for an object to belong to me, it must have been founded by me. It is totally mine only if I have founded it in its totality. The only reality that belongs entirely to me is, therefore, my act.[23]

It follows then that action is the locus of human identity: to be human is to act, and moreover, to be human is to act towards, to destine one's action. As a consequence, one is in a state of constant transcendence, through this action. "I am not a thing, but a project of self toward the other, a transcendence."[24] Citing the Gospels, Beauvoir explains by analogy her claim that she becomes a transcendence, someone who exceeds her own facticity, as a "spontaneity that desires, that loves, that wants, that acts" and, in so doing, she creates her singular relationship to the world:

---

22 Beauvoir, *Pyrrhus and Cineas*, 92.
23 Beauvoir, *Pyrrhus and Cineas*, 93.
24 Beauvoir, *Pyrrhus and Cineas*, 93.

> When the disciples asked Christ: who is my neighbour? Christ didn't respond by an enumeration. He told the parable of the Good Samaritan. The latter was a man abandoned on the road: he covered him with his cloak and came to his aid. One is not the neighbour of anyone; one makes the other a neighbour by making oneself his neighbour through an act.[25]

However, she observes that although my garden is mine by virtue of my cultivation of it, she is aware of those who do not act in sincere engagement, but rather "contents himself with pretenses,"[26] living a cautious and limited existence, focusing on fleeting pleasures of the moment. Beauvoir considers the pleasures of the Instant, of "Rest," and argues that this is not a worthy destiny for our action, because to be perpetually at rest is to tear oneself away from the world, to dwell in a meaningless ennui. This corresponds to her interpretation of Heidegger's claim that "Man is a being of faraway places," where humans are "constitutively oriented toward something other than himself [sic]. He is himself only through relationships with something other than himself,"[27] even in the apparent stillness of rest, where one's imagination and thought is also elsewhere at the same time. More than once, she argues that "rest," like "Paradise," is a closed and airless space, one that corresponds to the risk of knowledge, to the risk of that which is preserved safe and sound, unscathed. One only seeks rest momentarily, when one "lacks imagination,"[28] after which one will, if Pyrrhus, "hunt, he will legislate, he will go to war again"[29] because,

> One cannot fulfill a man; he is not a vessel that docilely allows himself to be filled up. His condition is to surpass everything given. Once attained, his plenitude falls into the past, leaving that "constant emptiness of the future [*creux toujours futur*] of which Valéry speaks gaping open.[30]

As she will argue in *The Second Sex*,[31] the particulars of a human being's existence are "made," not born, out of their ontological freedom. There is no predetermined "nature" by which we are determined beyond the bare facticity of our animality. She asserts that what each human being makes

---

25 Beauvoir, *Pyrrhus and Cineas*, 93.
26 Beauvoir, *Pyrrhus and Cineas*, 93.
27 Beauvoir, *Pyrrhus and Cineas*, 98.
28 Beauvoir, *Pyrrhus and Cineas*, 98.
29 Beauvoir, *Pyrrhus and Cineas*, 98.
30 Beauvoir, *Pyrrhus and Cineas*, 98.
31 See Beauvoir, *The Second Sex*, wherein her main philosophical argument is the interrogation of identity – in this case, gender roles.

herself into is an open question, and is, logically, one that can only ever be ascribed to the individual in question. In this way, she is not a "being" to be "filled" by outside actions or exhortations. This infers that as there is no ordering "form" for the human being, there is no presence, no teleological resting place: she is always in motion. Thus, the "instant" of pleasure, illusory and insubstantial, is not a satisfactory destination.

From her observation that once attained, "plenitude falls into the past," it follows that ends are beginnings: the justification for the project: "The notion of end is ambiguous, since every end is a point of departure at the same time. But this does not prevent it from being seen as an end. Man's freedom resides in this power."[32] The dialogue between Pyrrhus and Cineas hinges on Cineas' objection that Pyrrhus only goes forth to conquer that he may return, so why bother in the first place? Man "cannot find rest, and yet what is this movement that leads him nowhere?"[33] Beauvoir argues that the finite condition of our projects does not disqualify them:

> Pyrrhus is not leaving in order to return: he is leaving in order to conquer. That undertaking is not contradictory. A project is exactly what it decides to be. It has the meaning that it gives itself ... Each man decides the place he occupies in the world, but he must occupy one.[34]

One cannot destine oneself toward infinity because Infinity denies "those who unite me to this singular minute, to this singular corner of the earth."[35] Similarly, one cannot destine oneself towards a "universal truth, "since "my own self is abolished within the universal."[36] This is where Beauvoir first departs from Hegel's dialectic, rejecting his metaphysical premise, in which appearance is merely the given, historically situated "clothing" for the universal "*geist*": "Hegel declares in vain that individuality is only a moment of the universal becoming. If this moment, as unsurpassed, had no reality, then it should not even exist in appearance; it should not even be named."[37] For Beauvoir, the only truth that the human being can know is found in the moments of her singular and contingent existence. The idea of the universal leaves no room for the particular and contingent.

---

32  Beauvoir, *Pyrrhus and Cineas*, 99.
33  Beauvoir, *Pyrrhus and Cineas*, 102.
34  Beauvoir, *Pyrrhus and Cineas*, 100.
35  Beauvoir, *Pyrrhus and Cineas*, 101.
36  Beauvoir, *Pyrrhus and Cineas*, 101.
37  Beauvoir, *Pyrrhus and Cineas*, 101.

Her critique of the category of the "universal" also applies to the concept of God. To those who suggest God is a worthy end for one's actions, she observes that, according to the theological claim that God is infinity and plenitude, "The perfection of his being leaves no place for man,"[38] neither logically, in time or space, or ontologically. Man's freedom and transcendence is cancelled by such a conception. Or, if God wills that we destine ourselves to him, that we are a project not yet realized in the project of himself, Beauvoir concurs with Angelus Silesius, that "God needs me as I need him."[39] Here, Beauvoir is arguing the logical impossibility of human volition having any meaning if the account of theological metaphysics, that God is the totality, is tested against the experience of a specific living person. Following this inference, against those who would argue that "humanity" is a worthy end for our acting, she argues that "humanity" is a myth: there are only individuals. "Humanity is a discontinuous succession of free men who are irretrievably isolated by their subjectivity."[40] Against an apparent "Hegelian Optimism," she reasons that "it must be established that the synthesis effectively conserves the thesis and the antithesis that it surpasses; each man must be able to recognize himself in the universal that envelops him."[41] She counters that all that is preserved of the singular individual in Hegel is,

> precisely his facticity. The truth of a choice is the living subjectivity that makes it a choice in the end, and not the fixed fact of having chosen. Hegel retains only this dead aspect. As long as he falls into the world as a thing passed by and surpassed, man cannot find himself there. On the contrary, he is alienated there. One cannot save a man by showing him that the dimension of his being by which he is a stranger to himself and an object for others is conserved.[42]

So too, for those "floating in Hegelian ether, neither the life nor the death of these particular men seems important to us."[43] Consequently, there is no "Universal point of view," as no one individual is universal and "one cannot have a point of view other than his own."[44]

---

38 Beauvoir, *Pyrrhus and Cineas*, 102.
39 Beauvoir, *Pyrrhus and Cineas*, 104.
40 Beauvoir, *Pyrrhus and Cineas*, 109.
41 Beauvoir, *Pyrrhus and Cineas*, 111.
42 Beauvoir, *Pyrrhus and Cineas*, 112.
43 Beauvoir, *Pyrrhus and Cineas*, 112.
44 Beauvoir, *Pyrrhus and Cineas*, 112.

Having shown the deficiencies of infinity, God, pleasure and humanity as destinations for human action, Part 2 begins by affirming the appeal of the other: "But the other is there, before me, closed upon himself, open onto infinity. If I destined my actions to him, wouldn't they also take on an infinite dimension?"[45] The governing question becomes "what then do we expect from others?"[46] and, by implication, what do they expect of us?

Not devotion, which often takes on "an aggressive and tyrannical shape," without and against the other.[47] Devotion cannot be *for* the other because as argued earlier, "one cannot fulfill a man:"[48] "I am not the one who founds the other; I am only the instrument upon which the other founds himself. He alone makes himself be by transcending my gifts."[49] Here Beauvoir navigates the difficulty of ambiguity, insisting on the singular, particular existence of each individual and on her necessary and incontrovertible ontological freedom, an individual who alone can "found" or justify herself, who at the same time serves as an instrument for the other who finds her "gifts" – her projects – suitable for taking up as his or her own. If one accepts this paradox, she argues, then one accepts that we can do nothing for others: they can only do things for themselves. We can provide the occasion, but only each individual in this conception can act out the movement of her own human existence. She concludes that "the fundamental error of devotion is that it considers the other as an object carrying emptiness in its heart that would be possible to fill."[50] The same applies to an ethics of self-interest, which assumes "an emptiness was there the first, in me or in another, and that I would not have been able to act if the place for my action had not been already carved out."[51]

Instead, Beauvoir enjoins us to accept the ambiguity of our human condition and our human relationships:

> In enlightened, consenting gratitude, one must be capable of maintaining face to face these two freedoms that seem to exclude each other: the other's freedom and mine. I must simultaneously grasp myself as object AND as freedom and recognize my situation as founded by the other, while asserting my being beyond the situation.[52]

---

45 Beauvoir, *Pyrrhus and Cineas*, 116.
46 Beauvoir, *Pyrrhus and Cineas*, 117.
47 Beauvoir, *Pyrrhus and Cineas*, 118.
48 Beauvoir, *Pyrrhus and Cineas*, 121.
49 Beauvoir, *Pyrrhus and Cineas*, 121.
50 Beauvoir, *Pyrrhus and Cineas*, 122.
51 Beauvoir, *Pyrrhus and Cineas*, 123.
52 Beauvoir, *Pyrrhus and Cineas*, 123.

Instead of Hegel's "play of forces" which have emerged from struggle to recognition of their mutual dependence, Beauvoir affirms "enlightened, consenting gratitude." It is enlightened in the recognition of the ambiguity of every human being, "these two freedoms that seem to exclude each other: the other's freedom and mine," who are both always "object AND freedom," and by whom each is situated in her own specific context. "Consenting gratitude" implies acceptance of the ambiguity of each individual's condition as well as the ambiguity of their relationship. She argues, "we must know that we never create anything for the other except points of departure, and yet we must want them for ourselves as ends."[53] The gratitude flows from the fact of being faced by another human freedom, one who may justify my actions by founding her own actions out of mine. A reciprocal respect supports the one by the other. The gratitude also flows, by inference, from the fact that "a man would be nothing if nothing happened to him, and it is always through others that something happens to him, starting with his birth."[54] However, it must be selflessly given, without any thought of return. "It is not a matter of paying off a debt here ... A lucid generosity should guide our actions,"[55] or else they become selfish and self-defeating, like devotion. This chimes with Derrida's argument in *The Gift of Death*, that unless one gives unconditionally, one is still enclosed in a restrictive economy, which undermines the gift from within as soon as calculability enters.

Recognizing opposition and violence in the world, she notes, "And if I can do nothing for a man, I can do nothing against him either,"[56] because violence does not touch the ontological freedom of the person. One remains free, even to the extreme of choosing death rather than unjust suffering. This is not an endorsement of violence, but rather an illustration of the location of freedom – in the consciousness and will of the individual. In this sense, "we are therefore never anything but an instrument for the other, even when we are an obstacle, like the air that supports Kant's dove while resisting it."[57] Concluding this section with a very Pauline question, "Must we, then, conclude that our conduct towards others does not matter?"[58] she observes "it is indifferent for him ... But it concerns me, it

---

53 Beauvoir, *Pyrrhus and Cineas*, 123.
54 Beauvoir, *Pyrrhus and Cineas*, 125.
55 Beauvoir, *Pyrrhus and Cineas*, 124.
56 Beauvoir, *Pyrrhus and Cineas*, 124.
57 Beauvoir, *Pyrrhus and Cineas*, 125.
58 Beauvoir, *Pyrrhus and Cineas*, 125.

is my conduct, and I am responsible for it,"⁵⁹ because "I am the facticity of his situation."⁶⁰ Thus, one is always implicated in the situation of the other, a play that resonates with Derrida's Abrahamic trope in *The Gift of Death*, that response always involves the sacrifice of an other, which both condemns us and lifts us into our humanity. As a human freedom, we are able to choose among the situations that face us. However, how does one choose? "What is my true relationship with the other?"⁶¹ Turning to the "errors of false objectivity,"⁶² she observes another plane of ambiguity, that "working for some often means working against others,"⁶³ a dilemma not resolved by working for the good of all, since this is a meaningless category. Arguing against the fallacy of an "objective point of view," she affirms the fact of our perceiving others as "objects" and perceiving ourselves alone "in our intimacy and our freedom as a subject."⁶⁴ To try to imagine the point of view of the other is impossible, as it would require me to "cease being me,"⁶⁵ and so cease to have any point of view worthy of the name. Therefore, my view of others is always already contaminated by my own subjectivity, another register of ambiguity to accept.

Moving from this premise, of the irrefutable fact of our singular point of view, she then argues that, "the other's freedom alone is capable of necessitating by being. My essential need is to be faced with free men."⁶⁶ Critiquing Hegel again, she claims that "it is not a matter of making recognized in us the pure abstract form of the self [*moi*], as Hegel intends,"⁶⁷ arguing that we are only realized as beings in the world through "my actions, my works, my life," through the projects we make exist in the world, projects through which we communicate with others. If we do nothing, there is no possibility for communication because there is nothing by which we can appeal to the other. Some people delude themselves or misrepresent themselves as having founded things that they have not: "the jay adorns himself in peacock feathers and the handsome Christian borrows Cyrano's voice under Roxanne's balcony."⁶⁸ In the end, it is Cyrano that Roxanne truly loves, and

---

59 Beauvoir, *Pyrrhus and Cineas*, 125.
60 Beauvoir, *Pyrrhus and Cineas*, 126.
61 Beauvoir, *Pyrrhus and Cineas*, 126.
62 Beauvoir, *Pyrrhus and Cineas*, 126.
63 Beauvoir, *Pyrrhus and Cineas*, 127.
64 Beauvoir, *Pyrrhus and Cineas*, 128.
65 Beauvoir, *Pyrrhus and Cineas*, 128.
66 Beauvoir, *Pyrrhus and Cineas*, 129.
67 Beauvoir, *Pyrrhus and Cineas*, 129.
68 Beauvoir, *Pyrrhus and Cineas*, 129.

Christian, having "founded" nothing in this relationship gains nothing. "I take on shape and existence only if I first throw myself into the world by loving, by doing."[69] The "objects" that proceed from this loving and doing are the occasion for communication with the other. These objects are, however, contingent: "there are endeavours that extend over an entire life; others are limited to an instant, but none express the totality of my being since this totality *is not*,"[70] with the result that "we exist for others only insofar as we are present in our actions, and therefore in our separation."[71]

With whom does one want to communicate these separate endeavors, and what does one expect? Ideally, one wants one's projects to be taken up by an other who will appropriate it and thereby provide the conditions for this project to transcend me. "Truly, in order for the other to possess this power of making the objects that I founded necessary, I must not be able to transcend him in turn."[72] The other who takes up my project must herself, in "enlightened, consenting gratitude," turn every finite end of her own willing into a new point of departure, lest the other "appears to me as limited or finite, [and] the place he creates for me on earth is as contingent and useless [*vaine*] as himself."[73] In other words, the other must not only respond to the appeal of my project: the other must acknowledge and accept her ontological freedom and the moral freedom that it enjoins, an observation that will become the focus of *The Ethics of Ambiguity*:

> For I must have freedom facing me. Freedom is the only reality that I cannot transcend. How can one surpass what is constantly surpassing itself? If a being appears to me as pure freedom, if he is capable of founding himself entirely by himself, he can also justify what I have founded by taking it on as his own.[74]

The ambiguity of this argument is piquant. On the one hand, Beauvoir's human being is the being who is always becoming, always loving and acting in freedom, and so passing – temporally, materially, emotionally, intellectually – beyond the instant into the unfixed future. At the same time, one can, if lucid, appeal to another free human whose own becoming, "constantly surpassing itself," becomes the only logical absolute available.

---

69 Beauvoir, *Pyrrhus and Cineas*, 130.
70 Beauvoir, *Pyrrhus and Cineas*, 130.
71 Beauvoir, *Pyrrhus and Cineas*, 130.
72 Beauvoir, *Pyrrhus and Cineas*, 130.
73 Beauvoir, *Pyrrhus and Cineas*, 130.
74 Beauvoir, *Pyrrhus and Cineas*, 131.

Because we are faced with several freedoms, freedoms which "do not agree among themselves,"[75] we are faced with the necessity of choosing to whom we will respond, and by extension, appeal. The point of this observation is to insist that the justification offered to us by others who take up our projects is only valid while it is taken up – while it is lived and living. Nothing is "justified simply because they are written down in history."[76] The objects we create and throw into the world "will be saved only if others found a future that envelops it by surpassing it, and only if new objects choose it in the past for a future,"[77] a sentiment that resonates with Derrida's figure of inheritance and the obligations it enjoins us to, by responding – pledging again – to that which we inherit, to that which lives in the inheritance.[78] Thus, we want to be recognized by those who will move our projects toward a future we can still recognize as our own: "the project by which others confer necessity upon me must also be my project,"[79] again evoking an ambiguity at the heart of this schema, in which "I" am a free and willing subject whose project is taken up by an other to whom I am an object, and will appropriate my project into their own. We can respect those whose projects do not appeal to us, but we can only appeal "to the men who exist for me, and they exist for me only if I have created ties with them or if I have made them into my neighbours."[80]

> So here is my situation facing others: men are free and I am thrown into the world among these foreign freedoms. I need them because once I have surpassed my own goals, my actions will fall back upon themselves, inert and useless, if they have not been carried off toward a new future by new projects.[81]

She acknowledges that the hope that her projects will always be extended and so achieve absolute transcendence is vain, but she will continue the struggle nevertheless, because she wants to achieve *being*. In this text, the condition of *being* seems to be a condition of being recognized and justified by an other free consciousness. To the extent that one's project is adopted by the other, one enjoys *being*.

---

75  Beauvoir, *Pyrrhus and Cineas*, 131.
76  Beauvoir, *Pyrrhus and Cineas*, 131.
77  Beauvoir, *Pyrrhus and Cineas*, 132.
78  See Derrida, *Spectres of Marx*, "Exordium," xvi f.
79  Beauvoir, *Pyrrhus and Cineas*, 133.
80  Beauvoir, *Pyrrhus and Cineas*, 135.
81  Beauvoir, *Pyrrhus and Cineas*, 135.

> To seek to be is to seek *being* because *there is no* being except through the presence of a subjectivity that discloses it, and it is necessarily from the heart of my subjectivity that I rush towards it.[82]

She will continue to struggle, again, in "enlightened, consenting gratitude" in order that "free men," who must "love it, want it, and prolong it" can "give my actions and my works their necessary place."[83] The key here is that the other does so *freely*, and this requires respect: "Respect for the other's freedom is not an abstract rule. It is the first condition of my successful effort. I can only appeal to the other's freedom, not constrain it."[84] This necessary respect is reciprocal and so enjoins *rapport*: "But in order for this rapport to be established, two conditions must be met. First, I must be allowed to appeal."[85]

*Rapport* is a precise term for this relationship between human beings, etymologically derived from *rapporter* – to bring back: we reach out, give and receive, each brings back from the other. Beauvoir observes that some others may try to silence or stifle or suppress an individual voice, and with that, their being, against which one is justified in struggling. Secondly, "I must have before me men who are free *for me*, who can respond to my appeal,"[86] acknowledging the reciprocity necessary to this human foundation for meaning. Not only must these others be free to respond to my appeal, they must also be peers. Here, she argues that while violence is a fact of our world, and violence cannot touch the ontological freedom of the other, the man to whom one does violence "is not my peer, and I need men to be my peers,"[87] looking forward to Derrida's "culture of universalizable singularities" again. According to this premise, that in a world of free individuals, they may appeal to one another and so see their projects transcend themselves, it entails that there is no final goal or success possible, since "our goals are never anything but new points of departure," and even then, not all finite goals are achieved. Therefore, "we must assume our actions in uncertainty and risk, and that is precisely the essence of freedom."[88] It is also precisely the essence of faith. "Freedom is not decided with a view to a salvation that would be granted in advance. It signs no

---

82 Beauvoir, *Pyrrhus and Cineas*, 136.
83 Beauvoir, *Pyrrhus and Cineas*, 136.
84 Beauvoir, *Pyrrhus and Cineas*, 136.
85 Beauvoir, *Pyrrhus and Cineas*, 136.
86 Beauvoir, *Pyrrhus and Cineas*, 137.
87 Beauvoir, *Pyrrhus and Cineas*, 138.
88 Beauvoir, *Pyrrhus and Cineas*, 139.

pact with the future."⁸⁹ And yet, in another register of ambiguity, "I act only by assuming the risks of that future. They are the reverse of my finitude, and I am free in assuming my finitude."⁹⁰ By implication, one can only assume one's freedom by action: "man can act; he must act. He is only in transcending himself. He acts in risk and failure. He must assume the risk. By throwing himself toward the uncertain future, he founds his present, with certainty."⁹¹

Returning to her opening dialogue, Cineas is given leave to ask, "And after that?" reminding us of his initial critique of Pyrrhus. Rather than conclude that all is vanity, Beauvoir affirms that Cineas' question has merit, in that it performs a reflection. Reflection is valuable in that it reveals that "every project leaves room for a new question ... It releases me from the illusion of false objectivity."⁹² Reflection allows one the "enlightened, consenting" attitude required to assume one's freedom, and a clear view of the absolute singularity and separateness of others at the same time that we face each other as the conditions for each other's meaning: "In order to be recognized by them, I must first recognize them. Our freedoms support each other like the stones in an arch, but an arch that no pillars support. Humanity is entirely suspended in a void that it creates itself by its reflection on its plenitude."⁹³ Thus, the essay concludes that both action and reflection are necessary: reflection, which can only ever spring from a particular point of view, denies nothingness and affirms plenitude in its very existence; action throws us towards others, others who are the condition and promise for existential meaning. "Man knows nothing other than himself and cannot even dream of anything that is not human. To what can he therefore be compared? What man could judge man? In whose name would he speak?"⁹⁴

This lengthy review of Beauvoir's *Pyrrhus and Cineas* gives insight into some of the more abbreviated claims of *The Ethics of Ambiguity*. Most of the themes of the former are present in the latter, as both texts gravitate toward an articulation of ethics within an existential context. For example, the definition of the human being – as a "freedom" who "acts," and for whom meaning is only found when others take up our acts – so carefully developed in *Pyrrhus and Cineas* – is only briefly stated in *the Ethics of*

---

89  Beauvoir, *Pyrrhus and Cineas*, 139.
90  Beauvoir, *Pyrrhus and Cineas*, 139.
91  Beauvoir, *Pyrrhus and Cineas*, 139.
92  Beauvoir, *Pyrrhus and Cineas*, 139.
93  Beauvoir, *Pyrrhus and Cineas*, 140.
94  Beauvoir, *Pyrrhus and Cineas*, 141.

*Ambiguity*. So too is her argument for the necessity of acknowledging the human realm as the only possible site for human meaning, and the relationship between humans as the necessary condition for this. However, *The Ethics of Ambiguity* is more explicitly focused on the question of "how one ought to act," implicitly addressing the critics of "existentialism" and, more particularly, those critics of Sartre who claim that existentialism is a moral relativism devoid of ethics.[95] In meeting this criticism, Beauvoir spends considerable space describing the existential consciousness in the context of the European philosophical tradition before analyzing its moral implications.

She appeals immediately to this tradition in Part I, "Ambiguity and Freedom," invoking Montaigne in order to describe the ambiguity of the human condition: "'The continuous work of our life,' says Montaigne, 'is to build death.'"[96] She launches her thesis of ambiguity from this quotation, that the human condition is that of living only to die; conscious yet "crushed by the dark weight of things"; subject and object, singular yet a member of a collective, "useless passion." The history of philosophy according to Beauvoir, following Nietzsche, is a history of eluding the truth of this ambiguity and devising ethics on the basis of falsification of our true condition: "They have striven to reduce mind to matter, or to reabsorb matter into mind, or to merge them within a single substance."[97] Those "consoling ethics" emanating from these metaphysics either exhort the denial of the body in favour of a later spiritual reward, or recommend a yielding to the moment by engulfing oneself in it, only highlighting "the disorder from which we suffer."[98] Beauvoir dismisses the evasions and misrepresentations of metaphysics, and instead advises: "Let us assume our fundamental ambiguity. It is in the knowledge of the genuine condition of our life that we must draw our strength to live and our reason for acting."[99]

---

95 Beauvoir assumes her reader is aware of the public discourse on "existentialism" in the initial post-war period, and so does not name names. However, from her autobiography, and Edward Baring's recent study of the young Derrida, it seems likely she refers to Henri Lefevbre, Jacques Maritain, and to a lesser extent, Gabriel Marcel as those who accuse existentialism of being morally relativist, and ethically bankrupt. See Baring, *The Young Derrida and French Philosophy*, Chapter 1, "Humanist Pretensions," for a historical analysis of the political and intellectual context for Sartre's 1946 lecture, "Existentialism is a Humanism."

96 Beauvoir, *The Ethics of Ambiguity*, 7.

97 Beauvoir, *The Ethics of Ambiguity*, 8.

98 Beauvoir, *The Ethics of Ambiguity*, 8.

99 Beauvoir, *The Ethics of Ambiguity*, 9.

Asserting that existentialism has always been a philosophy of ambiguity, from Kierkegaard through Sartre, Beauvoir takes on the main criticism of existentialism, that it is "a philosophy of the absurd and of despair."[100] Beauvoir uses this observation and Sartre's declaration that man is a "useless passion" to argue for the necessity of an existential ethics. Here, assuming a familiarity with her existential claim that human beings possess neither a determined nature nor are destined to a pre-determined end, she argues that the "failure" implicit in the human as a "useless passion," the failure to ever achieve any absolute satisfaction in a world now emptied of metaphysics, is the necessary condition for *any* ethics: "without failure, no ethics." Citing Hegel, she observes his argument that "moral consciousness can exist only to the extent that there is a disagreement between nature and morality. It would disappear if the ethical law became the moral law."[101] Thus, not only does the existential acknowledgement of ambiguity and, ultimately, failure provide the conditions for the development of an ethic, at the same time, such an acknowledgement is also the acknowledgement of the undetermined freedom of the human being.

Turning specifically to Sartre's *Being and Nothingness*, she admits that it insists "above all on the abortive aspects of the human adventures."[102] However, she finds in its last pages an opening "for the perspective of ethics" which she intends to pursue, in Sartre's claim that "'man is a being who *makes himself* a lack of being *in order that there might be* being.'"

Kristana Arp has taken up Sartre's quotation in some detail, partly to argue for Beauvoir's intellectual independence from his philosophy. According to Arp, this quotation from Sartre should be understood in his text and in Beauvoir's as an inflection of Husserl's thesis about human intentionality. "In Husserl's terms, consciousness constitutes the meaning of objects in the world, and the meaning of the world itself."[103] However, while Sartre draws an absolute distinction between "*en-soi*" and "*pour-soir*," that is – between consciousness and non-consciousness – in between which he claims there is no communication, Beauvoir's ontology is closer to Merleau-Ponty's. She "stresses the dark, submerged links between the non-conscious and the conscious more than he [Sartre] does."[104] Arp emphasizes that the "being" which Sartre observes we lack is "being" as constructed by consciousness. Thus, she reads Sartre's

---

100 Beauvoir, *The Ethics of Ambiguity*, 10.
101 Beauvoir, *The Ethics of Ambiguity*, 10.
102 Beauvoir, *The Ethics of Ambiguity*, 11.
103 Arp, *The Bonds of Freedom*, 51.
104 Arp, *The Bonds of Freedom*, 52.

ontology as proceeding from the position of consciousness imposing itself on the world. Beauvoir, by contrast, sees the world as impinging on consciousness, as something that exists apart from our consciousness, and as something to which we have a powerful desire to merge rather than dominate.[105] Arp argues that this nuance is an important premise in Beauvoir's ethic, that the "failure to realize this basic desire is not a loss but rather a gain. For by making ourselves a lack of being we remain at a distance from nature. Due to this distance the sky and water exist before us."[106] The Husserlian influence observed by Arp is helpful, but where I part company with her is both in her reading of what "being" connotes in the quotation in question, as well as the rather limited and binary interpretation of the "*en-soi*" or realm of being-to-be-disclosed. Certainly, both Beauvoir and Sartre engaged with Husserl and phenomenology, but as Arp and Weiss have argued, her phenomenology allies her more closely to Merleau-Ponty than Sartre.[107] Moreover, to regard the "*en-soi*" as an undefined "nature" excludes the fact of each specific person whose "being" one is driven to disclose. Arp does herself admit that both Sartre and Beauvoir use the term "being" in more than one way, and often without precision.[108] That said, I will suggest a reading here that acknowledges both Beauvoir's knowledge of the European metaphysical canon and her rejection of its teleology, if not its methods.

Beauvoir, seizing on Sartre's claim that "man is a being who *makes himself* a lack of being *in order that there might be* being," finds in this thought an affirmation, not only of Husserlian intentionality but also of human autonomy: "his passion is not inflicted on him from without. He chooses it."[109] This is further corroborated by her italicizing of the words "*makes himself,*" which we can infer should be read as an act of self-determination. The "failure" of man's passion is not a cause for unhappiness, but instead for a recognition that such passion can find "no external justification."[110] Man [sic] lacks *being*, which here suggests the soul or *geist* of the European metaphysical tradition, and all of its consolations. However, in acknowledging the absence of "*being*," in acknowledging the existential ambiguity of the human condition, the human being can disclose "being" – those situated,

---

105 Arp, *The Bonds of Freedom*, 53.
106 Arp, *The Bonds of Freedom*, 55.
107 Weiss, "Beauvoir and Merleau-Ponty: Philosophers of Ambiguity" in Musset and Wilkerson, *Beauvoir and Western Thought*.
108 Arp, *The Bonds of Freedom*, 52.
109 Beauvoir, *The Ethics of Ambiguity*, 11.
110 Beauvoir, *The Ethics of Ambiguity*, 12.

finite, singular individuals along with the actions which, as we have seen in *Pyrrhus and Cineas*, define them. Such "uprooting" of the human being from the world grants a distance for perspective, and allows all things to be disclosed. "Man makes himself a lack, but he can deny the lack as a lack and affirm himself as a positive existence,"[111] effectively trading the empty consolations of metaphysics for the vital and ambiguous truth of existing. Invoking Hegel, "it might be said that we have here a negation of the negation by which the positive can be re-established", but "rather than being a Hegelian act of surpassing, it is a matter of conversion."[112] By this she means to eliminate the problem in Hegel of surpassed terms "preserved only as abstract moments, whereas we consider that existence still remains a negative in the positive affirmation of itself," in that "the failure is not surpassed, it is assumed."[113] The negation of the negation can be read here as the acknowledgement that there is no "being," and as there is no "being" to be lacking in, there is no lack at all. Instead, there is existence, the state of living temporally, situatedly, singularly, and the acknowledgement of the lack of "being" emanates from the recognition of this condition. Conversely, to acknowledge the "lack" of metaphysical "being" is to affirm existence. Hence the "positive affirmation of itself." At the same time, such an acknowledgement in no way mitigates the uselessness of the passion that Sartre claims defines us. In this way then, "the failure is not surpassed; it is assumed." By parsing Sartre's definition of the human being, Beauvoir situates the conditions for the ethic she is going to propose and at the same time explicitly informs us that she is using Hegel's dialectic as a point of departure rather than an end, a strategy we have seen at work in *Pyrrhus and Cineas*.

On the basis of this existential perspective, in which the genuine person "will not agree to recognize any foreign absolute," Beauvoir argues, again following Nietzsche,[114] that since we cannot evaluate the meaning of existence, the only question worth asking is "whether he wants to live and under what conditions."[115] Each person bears responsibility for the actions

---

111  Beauvoir, *The Ethics of Ambiguity*, 13.
112  Beauvoir, *The Ethics of Ambiguity*, 13.
113  Beauvoir, *The Ethics of Ambiguity*, 13.
114  See Nietzsche, *Twilight of the Idols*, "The Problem of Socrates: 2," 1229. "One absolutely must reach out and try to grasp this astounding *finesse*, that the *value of life cannot be assessed*. Not by the living, since they are parties to the dispute – in fact, thy are the objects of contention, and not the judges; not by the dead, for another reason."
115  Beauvoir, *The Ethics of Ambiguity*, 15.

she undertakes in her freedom. In this, Beauvoir identifies another existential conversion, in "the tradition of Kant, Hegel and Fichte, who, in the words of Hegel himself, 'have taken for their point of departure the principle according to which the essence of right and duty and the essence of the thinking and willing subject are absolutely identical,'"[116] although for existentialism that identification resides in the freedom of human beings and not in some abstract essence. The question existentialist ethics face is how can the plurality of particular, singular separate persons, each acting out her own reality, "get together?"[117]

After an excursus in which she considers how Marxism can, like Christianity, disallow the responsibility of the individual, Beauvoir reassigns the meaning of "being." She lifts it out of its static, all-encompassing metaphysical construction and transforms it to signify the consciousness of *beings* in the world, beings whose lives are meaningful, to the extent that a conscious subject perceives and engages with them. One may accuse her of equivocation, but it is a reading consistent with her rejection of essentialism and embracing of phenomenology. Here, Beauvoir argues that "the original scheme of man is ambiguous: he wants to be, and to the extent that he coincides with this wish, he fails. All the plans in which this will to be is actualized are condemned; and the ends circumscribed by these plans remain mirages."[118] Here we find a different register for "being" than the ones suggested by Arp. Here we have a suggestion of desiring a register of "being" that is now "condemned" as "mirage," the old *ontos* of the European metaphysical tradition. If this understanding of "being" is accepted, then her claim – that we want to "be" in some absolute sense, but fail – is a precise expression of ambiguity: the human being desires (for a variety of reasons, most situational) to be united to a transcendent absolute other, and at the same time, realizes the impossibility of this and so fails. However, she continues, "man also wills himself to be a disclosure of being, and if he coincides with this wish, he wins, for the fact is the world becomes present by his presence in it."[119]

Disclosure implies and requires a certain "perpetual tension to keep being at a distance, to tear oneself from the world and to assert oneself as a freedom."[120] On the one hand, as there is no transcendent absolute *"being"* in which to submerge oneself, only "beings," the existential

---

116 Beauvoir, *The Ethics of Ambiguity*, 17.
117 Beauvoir, *The Ethics of Ambiguity*, 16.
118 Beauvoir, *The Ethics of Ambiguity*, 23.
119 Beauvoir, *The Ethics of Ambiguity*, 23.
120 Beauvoir, *The Ethics of Ambiguity*, 24.

position requires acknowledgement of this, tearing oneself from the mirage of totality; on the other hand, such a recognition is also a recognition of freedom, because "freedom is the source from which all significations and all values spring. It is the original condition of all justifications of existence."[121] Addressing the apparent contradiction of granting people an original freedom while admonishing them to act out of this freedom, Beauvoir argues that "to will oneself free is to effect the transition from nature to morality by establishing a genuine freedom on the upsurge of our existence."[122] Following Hegel's observation that there is no ethics without failure, she asserts that it is only in recognizing and embracing the ambiguities of existence – and its inherent failures – that one can become authentically moral. One is born free, but one can "evade this choice,"[123] and so remain stuck in unrealized ontological freedom.[124] It is only by consciously thrusting one's freedom toward something, towards a project, that one is justified or "founded." "But this justification requires a constant tension. My project is never founded: it founds itself,"[125] to the extent of its limited ends. Here is where the need for the other enters, because when engaging in one's projects, "the movement of my transcendence requires that I never let it uselessly fall back upon itself, that I prolong it indefinitely,"[126] a feat that can only concretely happen through the grace of others.

Beauvoir does not develop this theme until the end of Part II and the beginning of Part III. Her concern at the end of Part I is to address the question of why ontologically free persons do not necessarily embrace their freedom as the locus of their moral agency, and are sometimes caught in a situation which "preserves existence in its pure facticity but forbids it all legitimation."[127] Why do some choose, at what Beauvoir terms the "moment of justification,"[128] the options of bad faith and self deception rather than risk the freedom of authentic existence? In the latter case, Beauvoir locates moral evil, placing it squarely in the choices realized by free persons who are necessarily responsible for their actions. Whether one chooses to blindly or cynically obey the received tradition, one is always responsible,

---

121 Beauvoir, *The Ethics of Ambiguity*, 24.
122 Beauvoir, *The Ethics of Ambiguity*, 25.
123 Beauvoir, *The Ethics of Ambiguity*, 25.
124 Arp designates Beauvoir's account of freedom in three registers as ontological, moral and concrete freedom. See Arp, *The Bonds of Freedom*, 2–3; 54.
125 Beauvoir, *The Ethics of Ambiguity*, 26.
126 Beauvoir, *The Ethics of Ambiguity*, 27.
127 Beauvoir, *The Ethics of Ambiguity*, 31.
128 Beauvoir, *The Ethics of Ambiguity*, 41.

from the critical perspective of existentialism, for one's choices, choices which sometimes manifest in evil. She argues that existentialism is the only philosophy "in which an ethics has a place," observing that,

> it is because there are real dangers, real failures and real earthly damnation that words like victory, wisdom, or joy have meaning. Nothing is decided in advance, and it is because man has something to lose that he can also win.[129]

In making this claim, she again evokes the concept that ethics is only possible where an alternative – the unethical option – exists. It also presages Derrida's claim in "Faith and Knowledge," regarding the logic of auto-immunity:

> But the auto-immunitary haunts the community and its systems of immunitary survival like the hyperbole of its own possibility. Nothing in *common*, nothing immune, safe and sound, *heilig* and holy, nothing unscathed in the most autonomous living present without a risk of autoimmunity. As always, the risk charges itself twice, the same finite risk. Two times, rather than one: with a menace and with a chance. In two words, it must take charge of – one could also say: take trust in – the *possibility* of that **radical evil** without which good would be for nothing.[130]

This passage in Derrida, which reiterates the logic of the autoimmunity of contemporary "religion" also offers a similar logic to that expressed by Beauvoir regarding existential responsibility: both agree that the responsibility that instantiates the self produces meaning precisely because there is risk: of failure, of rejection, that is at the same time a possibility, "a menace and a chance." By the same logic, the good requires the possibility of evil for its identity as good, without which there could be no moral meaning.

When we relate this axiom to her anthropology of freedom, freedom is the condition of ethics in that it allows for the possibility of retreat from responsibility as well as the deliberate abrogation of it. Part II, "Personal freedom and Others," is her sustained critique of those who "slide incoherently from attitude to another."[131]

Citing Descartes, Beauvoir observes that one is not "free" as a child. Instead, the child is "cast into a universe which he has not helped to establish, which has been fashioned without him, and which appears to him as an

---

129 Beauvoir, *The Ethics of Ambiguity*, 34.
130 Derrida, "Faith and Knowledge," 82.
131 Beauvoir, *The Ethics of Ambiguity*, 34.

absolute to which he can only submit."[132] Eventually, however, each person arrives on the path to maturity at a moment of doubt, a moment of questioning: this is the moment of justification, where the "serious world" she has received from her caregivers collapses and the young person "is cast into a world which is no longer ready-made, which has to be made; he is abandoned, unjustified, the prey of a freedom that is no longer chained up by anything."[133] Faced with this confusing and dizzying situation, Beauvoir details five types of "bad faith" responses to this "moment of justification," in ascending order: the sub-man; the serious man; the nihilist; the adventurer; and the passionate man. Each of these "types" is guilty of varying degrees of bad faith, and its consequences: fear, abdication, withdrawal, cruelty, nihilism, narcissism. Each of these attitudes is unjustified due to their inability to fully and transparently assume responsibility. The last type, who is also the most redeemable, the "passionate man," may come to the vital choice of accepting his distance from the "object" he desires, rather than eliminating it through various kinds of domination.

In this discussion, Beauvoir begins to lay out conditions of our relationships to each other. First, she insists that it "is only as something strange, forbidden, as something free, that the other is revealed as an other. And to love him genuinely is to love him in his otherness and in that freedom by which he escapes."[134] Such an acknowledgement evokes Françoise in *She Came to Stay*, her terror at the discovery of the facticity and freedom embodied by Xavière. But here, Beauvoir moves beyond the initial shock expressed by Françoise, and reasons that this otherness is constituted by a liberating freedom, a freedom each one possesses and which each can inhabit. The distance of "otherness" is produced by this ontological freedom, the same freedom by which "I" as subject can enjoy and ultimately escape the impositions of an other, as well as accept their free generosity. Moreover, the being one seeks to disclose by understanding oneself as a lack of being must be *an other being*, if we are to avoid solipsism. Of course, in keeping with her consistent understanding of the ambiguity of our condition, we may acknowledge the utter otherness of the other, at the same time that we acknowledge that the other founds the meaning of our lives. "Thus we see that no existence can be validly fulfilled if it is limited to itself," since, as she argued at length:

---

132 Beauvoir, *The Ethics of Ambiguity*, 35.
133 Beauvoir, *The Ethics of Ambiguity*, 39.
134 Beauvoir, *The Ethics of Ambiguity*, 67.

> To will oneself free and to will that there be *beings* is one and the same choice, the choice that man makes of himself as a presence in the world. We can neither say that the free man wants freedom in order to desire being, nor that he wants the disclosure of being by freedom. These are two aspects of a single reality. And whichever be the one under consideration, they both imply the bond of each man with all others.[135]

This bond, this *religio* – to invoke another etymology of "religion" – is the bond that creates the condition for meaning. If our projects are to be more than solipsistic vanities, there must be other consciousnesses that can respond to their appeal. Against Bataille, who argues that each man, desiring to be All, sees others as "a limit, a condensation of himself," and Hegel, who argues "each consciousness ... seeks the death of the other,"[136] she observes that to hate the other, to struggle against the other is naive and self-defeating, because "if I were really everything, there would be nothing beside me; the world would be empty. There would be nothing to possess and I would be nothing."[137] If we accept this logic, in which the fallacy of European "identity logic" – the drive to sublate the other into a unity – is laid bare, then it follows that "Man can find a justification for his existence only in the existence of other men."[138] Beauvoir makes a similar argument for human relationships as the locus of meaning when she observes that *nothing happens to a person* without the involvement of an other, starting with our birth, and that this "happening" is the promise and locus of meaning. "I concern others and others concern me: there we have an irreducible truth."[139] For Beauvoir, the question that arises, if one accepts this claim, is this: among the many appeals that face you, which ones do you choose?

> To will oneself free is to will others free. This will is not an abstract formula. It points out to each person concrete action to be achieved. But the others are separate, even opposed, and the man of good will sees concrete and difficult problems arising in his relations with them.[140]

The necessity of choosing which *others* to respond to, treated at length in *Pyrrhus and Cineas*, is treated again here, but within a different context.

---

135 Beauvoir, *The Ethics of Ambiguity*, 70.
136 Beauvoir, *The Ethics of Ambiguity*, 70.
137 Beauvoir, *The Ethics of Ambiguity*, 70.
138 Beauvoir, *The Ethics of Ambiguity*, 72.
139 Beauvoir, *The Ethics of Ambiguity*, 72.
140 Beauvoir, *The Ethics of Ambiguity*, 73.

Part III of *The Ethics of Ambiguity* is at once a reiteration of the argument that human meaning can only arise as an appeal and response between free agents who are utterly separate to one another, *and* at the same time a polemic against various criticisms against existentialism. The latter changes the emphasis of Beauvoir's apologetics, and leads to a lengthy consideration of the antinomies of ambiguity regarding oppression and the violence that may accompany it. Nevertheless, she begins Part III, "The Positive Aspect of Ambiguity," by asserting again the inextricable engagement of each person with other persons in "a speaking world from which solicitations and appeals rise up. This means that, through this world, each individual can give his freedom a concrete content,"[141] a pre-emptive volley against the charge that existentialism can provide no concrete ethic. One is always situated in a particular time and space, and can only play out one's good will, or lack thereof, among situated and situating individuals.

Above all, Part III allows Beauvoir to argue coherently for what she terms several times as "salvation." Redeploying her Roman Catholic lexicon, Beauvoir asserts that if we accept the description of the existential human condition given here – that there is no given meaning or aim for one's existence – then the only response to this fact that can grant meaning to one's existence is the ethical response: to respond to the appeal of the other, which is also a promise to the other. In this way only can we be "saved" from a meaningless or solipsistic existence, from "mere facticity."

This response is a double movement: on the one hand, it is a positive affirmation of one's freedom and the responsibility this entails, in order to disclose being in our response to the other; on the other hand, it is the negative movement of rejecting oppression as it inevitably curtails one's own freedom in oppressing the freddom of the other. The oppressor is inevitably one of the failed "types," whose motive and operations she details in Part II. The oppressor is trapped in the solipsism of her fear or cruelty – another expression of fear. Beauvoir's ethic explicitly and logically excludes such solipsism since the entire value of this ethic – the validation by the other – requires the freedom of the other. Speaking to the claim that existentialism is an "individualistic ethics," she responds,

> This individualism does not lead to the anarchy of personal whim. Man is free; but he finds his law in his very freedom. First, he must assume his freedom and not flee it; he assumes it by a constructive movement: one does

---

141 Beauvoir, *The Ethics of Ambiguity*, 74.

not exist without doing something; and also by a negative movement which rejects oppression for oneself and others.[142]

As time-beings, the reality of our experience of time-conception is powerfully engaged in this theory. This response to the appeal of the other and of their projects validates past lives and promises to those living today. She says of the child, even those in impoverished and dispossessed circumstances, "he is the living affirmation of human transcendence: he is on the watch, he is an eager hand held out to the world, he is a hope, a project."[143] The future is infinite; the present is the moment of decision and action. But the past, although complete and non-negotiable, speaks to us, carries forward those promises which we can still embrace.

> One does not love the past in its living truth if he insists on preserving its hardened and mummified forms. The past is an appeal; it is an appeal toward the future which sometimes can save it only by destroying it."[144]

This appeal from the past, from the spectral, an appeal which Derrida figures as an injunction,[145] demands response, but not idolatry. To respond is to pledge again, but not blindly or uncritically.

Let us recall that Derrida describes the site of faith as the promise between us – to tell the truth, to believe the other, even though they may be lying – which is also the risk.[146] This faith, in Beauvoir, is located in the promise I carry for the other, by responding to the appeal of her project, by appropriating her project, in order that it and, by extension she herself, has meaning beyond her own existence, a meaning that enlivens my existence : "let them accord value to one another in love and friendship, and the objects, the events, and the men immediately *have* this value; they have it absolutely."[147] Above all, the promise of the response includes an affirmation of solidarity, that we are not merely and utterly separate, but that we can appeal to one another for affirmation, for meaning, and perhaps receive it. This appeal is not abstract, as Beauvoir tried to show in her novels. Witness Anne in *The Mandarins* returning from the edge of sui-

---

142 Beauvoir, *The Ethics of Ambiguity*, 156.
143 Beauvoir, *The Ethics of Ambiguity*, 102.
144 Beauvoir, *The Ethics of Ambiguity*, 95.
145 For one such discussion of this figure, see Derrida, *Spectres of Marx*, 8–9.
146 This summarizes the discussion of faith and response given in *The Gift of Death*, and "Faith and Knowledge," more fully explicated in Chapter 3 of this dissertation.
147 Beauvoir, *The Ethics of Ambiguity*, 158.

cide, forced downstairs into her living house by the sounds of her family in the garden, *appealing* to her.[148] The other is neither always the enemy, nor always of the same nature, but he or she is a force and the condition of one's situation. Invoking Kant's dove again, she observes,

> The resistance of the thing sustains the action of man as air sustains the flight of the dove; and by projecting himself through it he accepts its being an obstacle; he assumes the risk of a setback in which he does not see a denial of his freedom … These withdrawals and errors are another way of disclosing the world.[149]

Across the straits separating individuals, there sounds an appeal and a promise to which one can respond in risk, with faith. This is the only consolation available to us:

> 'Do what you will, come what may.' That amounts to saying in a different way that the result is not external to the good will which fulfills itself in aiming at it. If it came to be that each man did what he must, existence would be saved in each one without there being any need of dreaming of a paradise where all would be reconciled in death.[150]

Beauvoir's ethic requires faith between individuals, radically separated from and "other" to each other, who appeal to one another and who in their freedom may respond to each other. Each response bears the promise of a kind of salvation from the void, from solipsism, from meaninglessness and facticity. This is the same faith that Derrida valorizes against knowledge, the other source in that play called religion. Where does the other source, "knowledge," feature in Beauvoir's thought?

Knowledge, "always tempting," is the affect of the drive to gather and bind, of the desire for stasis and stillness. "Knowledge" is the sign of those conditions that one seeks to indemnify and preserve unscathed, *heilig*, holy. The desire for "knowledge" is inaugurated by that same desire that aims at union with the other, and which in this function is the source of faith. Philosophically, Beauvoir accepts the impossibility of such conditions. As we have seen, for Beauvoir, the human condition is paradoxical, ambiguous and contingent, a fact that must be embraced and accommodated. The condition that she repeatedly admits she longs for – that of an absolute union with an other – is also repeatedly denounced as impossible.

---

148 Beauvoir, *The Mandarins*, 761.
149 Beauvoir, *The Ethics of Ambiguity*, 81.
150 Beauvoir, *The Ethics of Ambiguity*, 159.

This longing, as she describes it in "The Mystic" and in which she draws close to Certeau's figure, is toward a Beloved who is largely absent. In her ethics, she has clearly reassigned the object of this longing to the custody of "others" and finds in this situation a possible site for the production of meaning, through the chain of appeal and response already detailed. To the extent that one's projects are ultimately finite, however, the satisfaction of one's desire in the response of the other is limited, "ordering a sequel of wanderings and pursuit," as Certeau so eloquently puts it.

Knowledge, for Beauvoir in agreement with Derrida, is impossible amid the contingencies and finitude of human life. Her ethic is structurally a repudiation of the drive to homogeneity and hegemony, even as she admits, like Derrida, to the temptation of "knowing." In this she may be read as an agent of auto-immunity – resisting the very truth she was enlisted to protect, the immune system attacked by auto-immunity. Keenly sensitive to the implications of ambiguity, Beauvoir exhorts her readers to accept that the "facticity" of life is meaningless apart from the human beings who bear the weight of the things of this world. On the other hand, the meaning that people create between them is itself contingent, borne aloft like the air beneath Kant's dove – in resistance and tension. In Beauvoir's philosophy, which is a radical departure from the dominant metaphysical tradition embedded in the scene of religion, "knowledge" has been iterated as a *sign* of that which is ultimately contingent and ambiguous. As such, "knowledge" cannot be preserved, rendered *heilig*, holy, unscathed, and thus does not constitute the occasion for a phantasm of authority to rule the castle or the house.

However, if Beauvoir has undermined the possibility of "knowledge" as such by her insistence on the logic of ambiguity, what of the machinery of autoimmunity? In Beauvoir's thought, in her resistance to metaphysics and to all totalizing doctrines, out of her disciplined commitment to the acceptance of ambiguity, the play of the scene of religion can be seen. The scene of religion, which she rejects and moves away from in its manifestations in the Roman Catholic institution and doctrine and the bourgeois economic and social matrix the Church supported, is redeployed again: the site of the One – here, an existential iteration of the "Other" every "I" appeals to – changes, from a divine absence to a human subject. This change undermines the authority which underwrites the bourgeois capitalist Catholic tradition which Beauvoir abandons, but it does not abrogate the structure of *faith* per se, and so we may read this as a case of the mechanism of resistance – in this case, the 20th century scene of religion and the forces attempting to gather and bind its citizens in the service of an indeminified economy – producing the very threat it seeks to prevent – here, Beauvoir's critical interrogation and wholesale replacement of its tropes with existential philosophy and ethics.

## Chapter 5

## A Moving Scene

This study has sought to think the philosophy of Simone de Beauvoir within a different reading of her situated context, the scene of religion, a fitting figure within which to think the philosopher of ambiguity. On the one hand, we read in Derrida that religion is not some discrete category of belief and practice but, rather, is the unseen structure of our contemporary world, the world of global technological capitalism that proceeds from the Roman Empire. We cannot begin the enormous task of analyses that this requires here, but I do want to sketch what this reading of religion entails. If the structure of the scene of religion requires the play between gathering and binding to a fixed unquestionable authority, in order to reproduce that authority, then the contemporary iteration of "authority" is now located in the "strange alliance" of global techno-capitalism, for example, in those heirs of the Abrahamic, the "God-given" democracy of the United States of America, the heart of the global capitalist hegemony or in its putative enemies, the Islamicist resistance movements in the Levant. Derrida suggests that the hegemony of this economic-political alliance mirrors the hegemony of the Latin Christian world, and demands of those it gathers and binds in its name faith in its authority. The authority to which one pledges faith is an expression of a metaphysical chain of meaning that reaches from the ancient Near East, of Greece, of Jerusalem, of Byzantium, of Rome to the present culture of global capitalism. The faith offered to the various iterations of metaphysical authority is the same faith that Abraham, once upon a time, had to prove in secret by sacrificing his beloved son. Today, the authority of global-techno-capitalism is framed as the only economic system that can enable our undefined "freedom," and the "salvation" desirable in this world. It enjoins, like its theological predecessors, the same command to indemnify and keep unscathed its precepts, practices and truths, and to sacrifice others, when necessary to prove faith, in order to keep those same truths indemnified. But while in its Roman iteration we are asked to believe in a dying and rising son of God, in exchange for a place in Heaven, today we are asked to believe in the lights of techno-capitalism, including those protocols for bringing human rights to the rest of the world, in exchange for a place in the heaven of consumption, even when it means sacrificing others, "in secret," without public discourse or acknowledgement, to effect this economy.

By allying the received tradition of "godliness" that infuses the American and other national myths with the dynamism of modern technocracy and capitalist expansion, the current global regime authorizes its power in the name of God and liberty, circulating in an "economy" that Derrida traces specifically to the Christian. Ironically, its power proceeds from that matrix of knowing and making we call technology, a technology that threatens many of the proclaimed precepts of a particular Christian theology, with its capacity for ending, prolonging and radically engineering lives: the techniques of therapeutic abortion, machine assisted breathing, stem-cell research, cloning, virtual reality etc. This technology also produces machines – smart phones, laptops, tablets and their attendant platforms – that serve to gather and bind at speeds unthinkable in the past, producing silos of the like-minded that now wreathe the planet in virtual camps of solidarity. The current rise of authoritarian leaders preaching ultra-nationalist and even fascist narratives can be directly linked to the explosion of social media. The reality TV personality who becomes president of the United States understands this implicitly. Even among those who suspect this new world order, the substance of this play remains hidden: the critique of those still moved by an "invincible hope for justice" try to tweak the machine in the hope of revolution. But there is no "outside" of capitalism today, not even in the last bastion of what is called "communism" – China. China may have collectivized its social ordering, but its economy increasingly resembles state-sanctioned capitalism, creating the same division between its classes that the revolution pretended to eliminate. In this global world order, there are fewer and fewer spaces free from the machinery that reproduces and indemnifies the hegemony of capitalism and its drive to unlimited growth with its attendant injustices. The same machines that are the drivers of economic success are now consuming all the oxygen in the room, leaving the world more and more "breathless," *sans parole*, as some of us watch from the crowded margins. The very real danger of the force of global capitalist technocracy is the mechanical drive toward a homogeneity unthinkable before the digital lights of our era illuminated the globe, a homogeneity that in its totalizing effects will extinguish all those movements necessary to a creative, generous and just living.

On the other hand, the play of the scene of religion throughout European history also arrives at the disclosure of ambiguity, instability, *différance*, as well as Beauvoir's ethic. Beauvoir's philosophy makes enormous demands, nothing less than revolutionary demands. She enjoins her readers, first, to reject the metaphysical absolutes of the European tradition, and its chain of truths: almighty God, the Good; the eternal; the absolute; the safe and sound, the holy, the same truth claims that continue to underwrite the global technological capitalist economy of today. She demands a rejection of those comforting illusions and instead that the ambiguity of our condition is engaged, ethically. She asks no less than the confrontation of what might be viewed as idolatry, the "ontologizing of remains," that inaccessible, unknowable "truth" that demands credit, credibility and fidelity from the faithful. She demands this be confronted because it is at best a misrepresentation, in that it ignores the ambiguity and, at worst, it is a driver of radical evil, wherever it justifies force on the basis of a "mystical authority." She demands, instead, that we found our selves in the recognition of our bond with the other, even if this also demands that we accept the ambiguity of this bond: that responding to some always involves the sacrifice of others. She demands that we accept there are no prescriptions for response except that we respect and enable the ontological and moral freedom of the other, because this is the necessary condition for our own freedom. This in turn demands a commitment, therefore, to a constant effort to negotiate each situation, because each one to whom we appeal and respond is a situated singularity.

She demands an acceptance of the proposition that faith both exceeds determinate "religions" and is itself founded on that which gives religion, or at least religiosity, its only redeeming value, inspired by a hope in justice promised in the undecidable horizon. She asks that we redirect the response, which is at the heart of the scene of religion, toward the other before us, the singular discrete irreplaceable others with whom we engage. This requires a radical re-imagining of society, where the tropes of homogenous ethical prescription – of law, order, authority, and truth – that are currently uncritically assumed and reproduced would be iterated in favor of the heterogeneous "culture of universalizable singulairites." This may not be possible, but it may still serve as an impossible precept for Beauvoir's ethic.

However, the critique of European metaphysics does not imply the negation of metaphysics as such, of the transcendence that may come for the bane and enlightenment of humanity. Just as faith founds all relationships, so too Derrida's claim that *"all sacredness and holiness are not necessarily, in the strict sense of the term, if there is one, religious."*[1] There may be a way to hold as special, to cherish that which moves between us and the world, but it will require the reconcilliation of that endless desire and the fact of the contingency, without binding one to a phantasm of authority. It may be possible that the sacred and the holy may also inhabit heterogeneity.

Is such an alternative desirable? Before moving on to the implications of the enabling of heterogeneity in Beauvoir's ethic, an unspoken ethical assumption at play in the contemporary practice of critical theory should be acknowledged. An implicit assumption in much of the discourse of contemporary philosophy, and particularly in that indebted to French "post-modern" philosophy, is that heterogeneity is preferable to homogeneity. One might assume that this is self-evident as a political proposition, when the consequences of extreme movements of homogeneity, such as political and social fascisms, are considered. It is easy to condemn irrational intolerance and the persecution of other human beings, simply for being different, usually in ways that do not interfere with others. On the other hand, when societies and their subsets act according to implicit and desirable agreements about social discourse and behavior, this is, at the mild end of the spectrum, a movement of homogeneity that most societies wish to retain. This raises the question about the necessary role of homogeneity as a social force in the binary of "same" and "different," which is also the binary of "self" and "other." While the critique of uncritically held normative homogeneities is necessary and reasonable, the bonds of culture are also necessary. Perhaps the possibility of a "culture of universalizable singularity," a hope that Beauvoir's ethic enables, can become part of this play.

Returning to the implications of Beauvoir's ethic for enabling heterogeneity, I have suggested that Beauvoir performs a movement of autoimmune resistance within the scene of religion she inherits. When she rejects the authority of the bourgeois Roman Catholic tradition, she at the same time affirms faith between free subjects as a foundation for meaning. She says she realized that "god was no longer relevant to me."[2] There are several registers of meaning for this declaration. Within the context of this

---

1 Derrida, "Faith and Knowledge," 48.
2 Beauvoir, *Memoirs of a Dutiful Daughter*, 137.

specific passage in *Memoirs of a Dutiful Daughter*, "god" is no longer relevant to Beauvoir as a divine accountant, who promises rewards in an afterlife for conforming to specific behaviors now because, she concluded, "his name would have to be a cover for nothing more than a mirage,"[3] whereas the earth was manifestly alive and beautiful to her. The other obvious register of meaning here is the inference that if there is no "god," then the source of meaning for someone, driven by a desire for union with another, must be that very "other" before them. As we have seen, Beauvoir is sensitive to this as a young university student, even when she still has not critiqued metaphysics as such. The mature philosopher later develops a logic of reciprocity, in which individuals provide a reciprocal context for the founding of the meaning of each other's projects and, ultimately, lives. "God" no longer justifies existence; only "I," in my appeal to and response from "thee," can found my life, and only if this "I" assumes the mantle of freedom and responsibility that Beauvoir argues is afforded to each person. Here, she seems to engage Derrida's suggestion that perhaps "god" might be regarded as that possibility of interiority, of consciousness and conscience, that I keep within, in secret. Heir to the 'self" that we have seen inaugurated in the scene of religion, refined and valorized in the various European "Enlightenments," Beauvoir meticulously affirms the implication of "self-authorization," while insisting that such "self-hood" is woven into the self-hood of others. Thus, within this particular intellectual thread of the 20th century scene of religion, the authority of the tradition, the authority of "god," is replaced by the situated singular self, one who accepts the ambiguity of the human condition, and the contingent and fragile conditions for meaning.

Beauvoir's iteration of the scene of religion, a scene of a self, driven by desire, played out in the tension between faith and knowledge, begs an examination of the trope of the autonomous subject that occupies the site of faith in her thought. If we follow Derrida and Certeau faithfully, the "machine" for the making of gods does not quit because of meta-critical insight, and the logic of *différance* is always already at play. First, there is the contestable concept of the autonomous subject: is an individual definitively free to assume responsibility for one's choices and actions? According to Beauvoir's own logic, echoed in Derrida[4] and Certeau,

---

3 Beauvoir, *Memoirs of a Dutiful Daughter*, 137.
4 Derrida in particular has written extensively on "self" and its "authorization" – *selbstdarstellung* – in his reading of Freud, in which his deconstructions inevitably undo the conceits of Freud's self-conception. See "Archive Fever;" "Freud and the Scene of Writing," and "To Speculate: On Freud." Certeau responds

she would answer "no," since we are "the facticity" and the "situation" of each other's lives, and can never be said to possess autonomy in an absolute way. Other critiques of this construct, from the social sciences and psychological studies, suggest, for example, that the group mind is ubiquitous, and difficult to resist; that our animal drives both trump and constitute all *ratios*.[5] According to this logic, the figure of the valorized autonomous subject, if indemnified, is already automatically being resisted and contested, sometimes for good, other times for evil. Which is to say, that we who inherit this possible human being – the possibility of the responsible subject – must accept that it is not "pure," nor absolute, nor "unscathed" as a location for meaning.

On the other hand, this entailment of her thought, that of the contingency of all projects and thus all meaning, is the great merit of Beauvoir's logic of ambiguity. In this, she foresees and accommodates the necessarily contingent and unstable nature of our projects, enjoining us to undertake them despite their unavoidable contingency, that we might appeal to the other who is the only possible foundation for meaning, in risk and love. There is an opening here for a more rigorous analysis of the role of her free and responsible subject in her discourse, for an interrogation of this figure. Nevertheless, I propose that because Beauvoir frames her philosophy within the basic premise of ambiguity, her "subject" is a viable site for faith, the faith that seeks to satisfy desire, at least temporarily, in the custody of our relationships.

As for knowledge – the figure of that which can be known in some static sense – this too is subject to her logic of ambiguity, to the play of call and response, between specific situated contingent persons. To be clear, with respect to the "serious" tradition she rejects, she nevertheless does not reject those figures in that tradition which still speak with a human wisdom and tenderness, only those absurdities that exhibit "force of law" without offering a corresponding justice for the fact of our singular freedoms.

In this context, it is important to recall that Beauvoir's philosophy always enjoins a response: after metaphysics, after disenchantment with progress and reason, what is the basis of meaning in a godless universe? What is our relationship to the others in this existentially conceived world?

---

more obliquely to this problem, but nevertheless engages in a psychological profile of "mystic" mentors in *Possession at Loudun* that suggest the play of the self as social construct.

5 For example, see Doris Lessing's reflection on the Milgram experiments called "Group Minds;" or Derrida's reading of Freud's *Beyond the Pleasure Principle* in "To Speculate: On Freud."

At the same time, her existential stance, as a reaction to the injunctions of the European scene of religion, honors that tradition – performatively and theoretically – even as it transcends and transforms it. No existentialism without a metaphysics-of-being to reject; no ambiguity without the tradition of knowledge and knowing to resist; no meaningful faith in the other without the tradition of faith in the Other. In other words, the existential justice her philosophy opens upon is itself an iteration of the same tradition it succeeds, and is in a logical way, a necessary development of the scene of religion.

The philosophy of Beauvoir, in harmony with Derrida and Certeau, does not negate or cancel the European inheritance in its resistance to its metaphysics. Both insist on inheriting the past, because it is only through our re-appropriation of those living projects that came before us that we can foresee a meaning for our own actions. But inheriting the past here cannot mean an uncritical reproduction of untenable ontologies and the tyranny of blind authority. Beauvoir's ethic is a response to that inheritance – an act of that originary faith that perpetuates the tradition of this civilization, a promise to believe in the other, even if the other misrepresents themselves and their truths. At the same time, this faith is also an act of an "invincible hope for justice," one that may appear to "a universalizable culture of singularities."

At stake in this study of Beauvoir's philosophy of ambiguity is the figure of religion. The "scene" offered in my reading of Derrida and Certeau may have its roots in the quotation from Bergson, that "the universe is a machine for the making of gods."[6] Interrogating religion as a scene – that is, as a play of forces enacted by human beings, subject to repetition and change, subject to disruption, vulnerable to autoimmunity and its violences – demonstrates the working of the "machine" that gathers and binds even while undoing that which it seeks to hold indemnified. This scene, as we have seen, is specifically situated, in the world, in its economy and politics and social structures, and is driven by two sources which exceed this scene. The theory that this scene affords undermines uncritical approaches to religion – those approaches that view it as something discrete, private, precious, and beyond rational analysis. On the other hand, it complements critically aware approaches by situating them in a meta-theoretical context. The figure of the scene of religion provides a site for understanding through the very mechanisms which constitute it – faith and knowledge – and contributes to the difficult and necessary task

---

6 Bergson, as quoted in Derrida, "Faith and Knowledge," 77.

of disentangling an inadequate concept of religion from its implications in our complex and troubled contemporary situation.

Locating the existential philosopher Beauvoir within this scene as an agent of its mechanisms at the same time that she resists its unjust constraints reveals a reinscription of faith as a category of human action. It offers faith as the promised fulfillment of the ancient prayer – "may I not be separated from thee" – as an opening for what may come, even justice. Her existential ethic anticipates Derrida's figure of messianicity: the logic of the binary orders it so. No rejection of "religion" that does not always already imply "religion."Consider this chain of logic offered by Derrida:

> Axiom: No to-come without heritage and the possibility of *repeating*. No to-come without some sort of iterability, at least in the form of a covenant with oneself and *confirmation* of the originary *yes*. No to-come without some sort of messianic memory and promise of a messianicity older that all religion, more originary than all messianism. No discourse or address of the other without the possibility of an elementary promise. Perjury and broken promises require the *same* possibility. No promise, therefore, without the promise of a confirmation of the *yes*. This *yes* will have implied and will always imply the trustworthiness and fidelity of a faith.[7]

What if we agree to revisit what is meant by religion, according to what is given here? Instead of signalling some unknowable, unattainable sacred category of beliefs and practices, a category casually deployed to explain and justify all manner of conflicts, oppression and violence in the world, what if religion is understood as that deep structure of appeal and response, reproduction and resistance, that operates in all aspects of our contemporary human world? What if this understanding of religion as a scene of gathering and binding as well as an act of that faith which enables justice were to be investigated, debated and embraced? Perhaps, then we might be able to step toward Beauvoir's vision: "If it came to be that each man did what he must, existence would be saved in each one without there being any need of dreaming of a paradise where all would be reconciled in death."[8]

---

7   Derrida, "Faith and Knowledge," 83.
8   Beauvoir, Ethics of Ambiguity, 159.

# Bibliography

Andrew, Barbara S. "Beauvoir's Place in Philosophical Thought." *The Cambridge Companion to Simone de Beauvoir*, edited by Claudia Card, 22-44. Cambridge: Cambridge University Press, 2003. https://doi.org/10.1017/CCOL0521790964.002

Arp, Kristana. *The Bonds of Freedom: Simone de Beauvoir's Existentialist Ethic*. Chicago: Open Court Press, 2001.

Bair, Deirdre. *Simone de Beauvoir: A Biography*. New York: Touchstone, 1990.

Bakewell, Sarah. *At the Existentialist Café: Freedom, Being and Apricot Cocktails*. Toronto: Knopf Canada, 2016.

Baring, Edward. *The Young Derrida and French Philosophy, 1945-1968*. Cambridge: Cambridge University Press, 2012. https://doi.org/10.1017/CBO9780511842085

Barnard, G. William. *Exploring Unseen Worlds: William James and the Philosophy of Mysticism*. New York: State University of New York Press, 1997.

Berghoffen, Debra. *The Philosophy of Simone de Beauvoir: Gendered Phenomenologies, Erotic Generosities*. New York: State University of New York Press, 1997.

Beauvoir, Simone de. *The Ethics of Ambiguity*. Translated by Bernard Frechtman. New York: Citadel Press, 1948, 1978.

— *The Mandarins*. Translated by Leonard M. Friedman. London: Fontana Books, 1957.

— *When Things of the Spirit Come First*. Translated by Patrick O'Brian. New York: Pantheon Books, 1982.

— *A Farewell to Sartre*. Translated by Patrick O'Brian. London: Andre Deutsch and Weidenfeld and Nicholson, 1984.

— *The Second Sex*. New York: Vintage Books Edition, 1989.

— *After the War: Force of Circumstance*. Translated by Richard Howard. Introduction by Toril Moi. New York: Paragon House, 1992.

— *After the War: Hard Times*. Translated by Richard Howard. Introduction by Toril Moi. New York: Paragon House, 1992.

— *The Prime of Life*. Translated by Peter Green. Introduction by Toril Moi. New York: Paragon House, 1992.

— *Letters to Sartre*. Translated by Quinton Hoare. New York: Arcade Publishing, 1993.

— *All Said and Done*. Translated by Patrick O'Brian. Introduction by Toril Moi. New York: Paragon House, 1993.
— *She Came to Stay*. London: Flamingo, 1995.
— *The Coming of Age*. Translated by Patrick O'Brian. New York: W.W. Norton & Co., 1996.
— *America Day by Day*. Translated by Carl Cosman. Berkeley: University of California Press, 1999.
— "Literature and Metaphysics." (1946) *Philosophical Writings*. Edited by Margaret Simons. Chicago: The University of Illinois Press, 2004.
— "*Pyrrhus and Cineas*" (1944) *Philosophical Writings*. Edited by Margaret Simons. Chicago: The University of Illinois Press, 2004.
— "What is Existentialism." (1947) *Philosophical Writings*. Edited by Margaret Simons. Chicago: The University of Illinois Press, 2004.
— *Memoirs of a Dutiful Daughter*. Translated by James Kirkup. New York: Harper Perennial Modern Classics, 2005.
Bocken, Inigo, ed. *Spiritual Spaces: History and Mysticism in Michel de Certeau*. Leuven: Peeters Publishers, 2013.
Caputo, John D. *The Prayers and Tears of Jacques Derrida*. Bloomington: Indiana University Press, 1997. https://doi.org/10.2307/j.ctt2005rjr
Certeau, Michel de. *The Mystic Fable*. Chicago: University of Chicago Press, 1992.
— *The Possession at Loudun*. Chicago: University of Chicago Press, 2000.
Cixous, Hélène. *Portrait of Jacques Derrida as a Young Jewish Saint*. New York: Columbia University Press, 2005.
Daigle, Christine and Jacques Colomb, eds. *Beauvoir and Sartre: The Riddle of Influence*. Bloomington: Indiana University Press, 2009.
Deranty, Jean Phillipe. "Adorno's Other Son: Derrida and the Future of Critical theory." *Social Semiotics* 16, no. 3 (2006): 421–33.
https://doi.org/10.1080/10350330600824011
Derrida, Jacques. "Différance." *Writing and Difference*. Chicago: University of Chicago Press, 1978.
— *Writing and Difference*. Chicago: University of Chicago Press, 1978.
— "Freud and the Scene of Writing." *Writing and Difference*. Translated by Alan Bass. Chicago: University of Chicago Press, 1978.
— *Dissemination*. Translated by Alan Bass. Chicago: University of Chicago Press, 1981.
— "To Speculate: On Freud." *The Postcard*. University of Chicago Press, 1987.
— "A Number of Yes." *Qui Parle* 2, no. 2 (1988): 118–33.
— "Force of Law: The Mystical Foundation of Authority." *Cardozo Law Review* 11 (1989-1990): 921–1048.
— *Spectres of Marx*. New York: Routledge, 1994.
— "Archive Fever: A Freudian Impression." *Diacritics* Vol. 25, No. 2 (1995), 9–63.
— *The Gift of Death* and *Literature in Secret*. Translated by David Wills. Chicago: University of Chicago Press, 1995; 2008.
— "*Sauf le Nom.*" *On the Name*. New York: Palo Alto: Stanford University Press, 1995.
— "Passions: An Oblique Offering." *On the Name*. Palo Alto: Stanford University Press, 1995.
— *The Work of Mourning*. London: University of Chicago Press, 2001.

— "Faith and Knowledge: The Two Sources of Religion at the Limits of Reason Alone." *Acts of Religion*. Edited by Gil Anidjar. New York: Routledge, 2002.
— *Learning to Live Finally: The Last Interview*. New York: Melville House, 2007.
Deutscher, Penelope. "Enemies and Reciprocities," MLN 119, no. 4 (2004): 656-71.
— *The Philosophy of Simone de Beauvoir: Ambiguity, Conversion, Resistance*. Cambridge: Cambridge University Press, 2008. https://doi.org/10.1017/CBO9780511490507
De Vries, Hent. *Philosophy and the Turn to Religion*. Baltimore: Johns Hopkins University Press, 1999.
Elliott, Dyan. *The Bride of Christ Goes to Hell. Metaphor and Embodiment in the Lives of Pious Women, 200-1500*. Philadelphia: University of Pennsylvania Press, 2012.
Evans, Jean and Celia E.T. Courie. "Towards Understanding Mystical Consciousness: An Analysis of a Text from Simone Weil." *Religion and Theology* 10, no. 2 (2003): 149-65. https://doi.org/10.1163/157430103X00024
Fabijancic, Ursula. "Le Deuxième sexe 1949-1999: Our Continuing Dialogue with Simone de Beauvoir." *Simone de Beauvoir Studies* 15 (1998-1999): 1-16. https://doi.org/10.1163/25897616-01501002
Fitzgerald, *The Ideology of Religion*. Oxford: Oxford University Press, 2003.
Frapp, Peter. Bibliography of Works by Jacques Derrida by Year (compilation in progress): 1994-2006. Webpage. http://hydra.humanities.uci.edu/derrida/jdyr.html. June 12, 2017.
Frijhoff, William. "Michel de Certeau (1925-1986) - A Multifaceted Intellectual." *Spiritual Spaces: History and Mysticism in Michel de Certeau*. Edited by Inigo Bocken. Leuven: Peeters Press, 2013.
Füssel, Marian. "Writing the Otherness - The Historiography of Michel de Certeau SJ," *Spiritual Spaces: History and Mysticism in Michel de Certeau*. Edited by Inigo Bocken. Leuven: Peeters Press, 2013.
Giard, Luce. "Michel de Certeau's Biography: petite bibliographie en anglais." Jesuites.com, February 5, 2006. Available at: http://www.jesuites.com/histoire/certeau.htm#bio. Website 12 March 2017.
Gothlin, Eva. "Reading Simone de Beauvoir with Martin Heidegger," in *The Cambridge Companion to Simone de Beauvoir*. Cambridge: Cambridge University Press, 2013, 36.
Green, Karen. "The Other as Another Other." *Hypatia: A Journal of Feminist Philosophy* 17, no. 4 (2002): 1-15. https://doi.org/10.1353/hyp.2002.0072
Haaglund, Martin. *Radical Atheism: Derrida and the Time of Life*. Palo Alto: Stanford University Press, 2008.
Heinämaa, Sara. "Simone de Beauvoir's Phenomenology of Sexual Difference." *Hypatia: A Journal of Feminist Philosophy* 14, no. 4 (1999): 114-32. https://doi.org/10.1353/hyp.2005.0029
Hegel, G.W.F. *The Phenomenology of Spirit*. [Selections] *Classics of Western Philosophy*. Eighth Edition. Edited by Steven M. Cahn. Indianapolis: Hackett Publishing Co., 2012.
Hobson, Marion. *Jacques Derrida: Opening Lines*. London: Psychological Press, 1998.
Hollywood, Amy. "Love Speaks Here: Michel de Certeau's *Mystic Fable*." *Spiritus: A Journal of Christian Spirituality* 12, no. 2 (2012): 198-206. https://doi.org/10.1353/scs.2012.0047
Holveck, Eleanore. *Simone de Beauvoir's Philosophy of Lived Experience. Literature and Metaphysics*. Lanham, MD: Rowman and Littlefied Publishers, 2002.

Janzen, Grace M. *Power, Gender, and Christian Mysticism*. Cambridge: Cambridge University Press, 1995.

Kamuf, Peggy. "Composition Displacement." *MLN* 121, no. 4 (French Issue) September 2006: 872–92. https://doi.org/10.1353/mln.2006.0095

Kippenberg, Hans. *Discovering Religious History in the Modern Age*. Princeton: Princeton University Press, 2002.

Kirkpatrick, Kate. *Becoming Beauvoir: A Life*. London: Bloomsbury, 2019.

Kugle, Scott. *Sufis and Saint's Bodies: Mysticism, Corporeality, and Sacred Power in Islam*. Chapel Hill: The University of North Carolina Press, 2007. https://doi.org/10.5149/9780807872772_kugle

Lecarme-Tabone, Eliane. "Introduction." *Mémoires d'une jeune fille rangée de Simone de Beauvoir* (Essai et dossier). Paris: Gallimard Collection Foliotheque, no. 85, 2000.

Lefebvre, Alexandre and Melanie White, editors, "Introduction." *Bergson, Politics and Religion*. Durham and London: Duke University Press, 2012.

Lessing, Doris. "Group Minds." *Prisons We Choose to Live Inside*. CBC Massey Lectures. Toronto: Perennial Paperbacks, 1987.

Llewelyn, John. *Margins of Religion: Between Kierkegaard and Derrida*. Bloomington: Indiana University Press, 2009.

Mahon, Joseph. *Simone de Beauvoir and Her Catholicism. An Essay on Her Ethical and Religious Meditations*. Dublin: Arlen House, 2002.

Martin, Craig. *Capitalizing Religion: Ideology and Opiate of the Bourgeoisie*. London: Bloomsbury Academic, 2014.

Masuzawa, Tomoko. *The Invention of World Religions or How European Universalism was Preserved in the Language of Pluralism*. Chicago: University of Chicago Press, 2005.

McCance, Dawne. *Derrida on Religion: Thinker of Difference*. Sheffield: Equinox Publishing, 2008.

— *Sleights of Hand*. Vernon, BC: The Kalamalka Press, 2009.

McCutcheon, Russell T. *Manufacturing Religion: The Discourse on Sui Generis Religion and the Politics of Nostalgia*. New York: Oxford University Press, 1997.

Mussett, Shannon and Sally J. Scholz. *The Contradictions of Freedom: Philosophical Essays on Simone de Beauvoir's The Mandarins*. New York: State University of New York Press, 2005.

— and William Wilkerson. *Beauvoir and Western Thought: from Plato to Butler*. New York: State University of New York Press, 2012.

Naas, Michael. "Comme si, comme ça": Phantasms of Self, State, and a Sovereign God." *Mosaic: An Interdisciplinary Critical Journal* 40, no. 2 (2007): 1–26.

— *Miracle and Machine: Jacques Derrida and the Two Sources of Religion, Science and the Media*. New York: Fordham University Press, 2012.

Nietzsche, F.W. *Twilight of the Idols* in *Classics of Western Philosophy 8th Edition*. Edited by Steven M. Cahn. Indianapolis: Hackett Publishing, 2012.

O'Brien, Wendy. *Simone de Beauvoir and The Problem of the Other's Consciousness: Risk, Responsibility and Recognition*. Unpublished dissertation. University of Waterloo, 2013.

O'Brien, Wendy and Lester Embree. *The Existential Phenomenology of Simone de Beauvoir*. Contributions to Phenomenology, Volume 4. Springer Netherlands, 2001. https://doi.org/10.1007/978-94-015-9753-1

Parker, Emily Anne. "Singularity in Beauvoir's *The Ethics of Ambiguity*." *The Southern Journal of Philosophy* 53, no. 1 (2015): 1–16.

Pippin, Robert B. *Hegel on Self-Consciousness: Desire and Death in the Phenomenology of Spirit*. Princeton: Princeton University Press, 2010. https://doi.org/10.1515/9781400836949

Said, Edward. *Orientalism*. New York: Vintage Books, 1979.

Sells, Michael A. *Mystical Languages of Unsaying*. Chicago: University of Chicago Press, 1994.

Siep, Ludwig, *Hegel and the Phenomenology of Spirit*. Translated by Daniel Smyth. Cambridge: Cambridge University Press, 2014.

Simons, Margaret A., ed. *The Philosophy of Simone de Beauvoir: Critical Essays*. Bloomington: Indiana University Press, 2006.

Smith, J.Z. *Imagining Religion. From Babylon to Jonestown*. Chicago: University of Chicago Press, 1982.

Taves, Ann. *Fits, Trances and Visions*. Princeton: Princeton University Press, 1999. https://doi.org/10.1515/9780691212722

— *Religious Experience Reconsidered*. Princeton: Princeton University Press, 2011.

Taylor, Mark C. *Erring: A Postmodern A/theology*. Chicago: University of Chicago Press, 1984. https://doi.org/10.7208/chicago/9780226169439.001.0001

Tidd, Ursula. "The Self-Other Relation in Beauvoir's Ethics and Autobiography." *Hypatia: A Journal of Feminist Philosophy* 14, no. 4 (1999): 163–74. https://doi.org/10.1111/j.1527-2001.1999.tb01259.x

Walker-Bynum, Caroline. *Fragmentation and Redemption*. Cambridge, MA: Zone Books, 1991.

— *Metamorphosis and Identity*. Cambridge, MA: Zone Books, 2005.

Weiss, Gail. "Beauvoir and Merleau-Ponty. Philosophers of Ambiguity." *Beauvoir and Western Thought from Plato to Butler*. Edited by Shannon M. Mussett and William S. Wilkerson. New York: State University of New York Press, 2012: 170–89.

# Index of Names and Select Titles by Author

Algren, Nelson 11; 15
Angela de Foligno 80
Angelus Silesius 20; 94
Arp, Kristana 103–7

Bair, Deirdre 7–12; 124
Baring, Edward 16–19; 52; 71; 102
Bataille, Georges 14; 110
Baudelaire, Charles 40
Beauvoir, George Bertrand de 7–9
Beauvoir, Simone de 7–17; 45; 71–86; 116; 124–8
  *A Farewell to Sartre* 112, n. 27
  *All Said and Done* 12; 21; 22; 66–9; 77; 83
  *America Day by Day* 11; 74; 116–17
  *Les Bouche Inutiles – Useless Mouths* 12
  *The Ethics of Ambiguity* 3; 5; 12; 17–20; 45; 62; 82–114; 123
  *Force of Circumstance: I and II* 11; 15; 66
  *L'Invitée – She Came to Stay* 11; 86–9; 109
  *Les Sang des Autres – The Blood of Others* 11–12
  *Les Deuxieme Sex – The Second Sex* 6; 12; 14; 20–21; 59; 66; 70–80; 84, n. 24; 92
  *Les Mandarins – The Mandarins* 66; 112–13
  *Les Temps Moderne* 11
  *Memoires d'une Jeune Fille Rangée – Memoirs of a Dutiful Daughter* 2; 10; 14; 20; 60–82; 119–20
  *Pyrrhus and Cineas* 11; 40–5; 82–110
  *The Coming of Age* 22
  *The Prime of Life* 11; 40; 66; 74–89
  *The Woman Destroyed* 12
  *Tout les hommes sont Mortels – All Men are Mortal* 12
  *When Things of the Spirit Come First* 11; 66–9; 81

Benviniste, Emile 38
Berghoffen, Deborah 13; 90
Bergson, Henri 13; 31–2; 52–3; 122
Bernard of Clairvaux 80
Brasseur, Francoise 7–9; 15

Camus, Albert 11; 16
Certeau, Michel de 20–27; 56–82; 114; 120; 122
  *The Mystic Fable* 1; 5; 20–26; 53–82
  *The Possession at Loudun* 20; 81
  *The Practice of Everyday Life* 26

Derrida, Jacques 16–57; 61–76; 83–5; 122–23
  "Faith and Knowledge: The Two Sources of Religion at the Limit of Reason Alone" 31–67; 108–12; 120–23
  "Force of Law" 19
  "Khora" 29–30; 50
  *Of Grammatology* 28
  "Passions: An Oblique Offering" 19
  "Sauf le Nom" 20; 50
  *Spectres of Marx* 19; 53–4; 99; 112
  *The Gift of Death* 19; 28–54; 96–7; 112
  "The Problem of Genesis" 18
  "To Speculate: On Freud" 53; 120–21
Descartes, Rene 61; 108

Eliade, Mircea 24
Elliot, Dyan 80

Fitzgerald, Timothy 25
Fussel, Marian 20; 57
Freud; Sigmund 48-56; 120-21

Giard, Luce 20

Heinamaa, Sara 13
Hegel, G.W.F. 11-13; 19-21; 29-31; 47; 55-61; 85-97; 103-10
  *Phenomenology of Spirit*
Heidegger, Martin 11; 13; 32; 92
Hollywood, Amy 6-7, n. 2; 14, n. 30; 22; 65, n. 1
Hussurl, Edmund 18-19; 103-4

Janzen, Grace 8, n. 51
Jeanne des Anges 81
John of the Cross 73; 78; 80

Kant, Immanuel 13; 30-3; 43; 50; 61; 96; 113-14
Kamuf, Peggy 28-9
Kippenberg, Hans 24, n. 1; 26
Kirkpatrick, Kate 12

Lanzman, Claude 11; 15
Lacan, Jacques 14; 20
Lecarme Tabone, Eliane 14; 66; 74

Lessing, Doris 121
Levi-Strauss, Claude 22

Madame Guynon 78
Mahon, Joseph 7, n. 2
Masuzawa, Tomoko 25-6
McCutcheon, Russell 24-5
Merleau-Ponty, Maurice 10-11; 19; 73; 103-4
Montaigne, Michel de 102

Naas, Michael 9; 51
Nietzsche, Frederick 13; 48; 50; 102; 105

O'Brien, Wendy 85

Pascal, Blaise 14; 66; 71
Patocka, Jan 33; 40-9

Sartre, Jean Paul 6; 10-19; 74-6; 82; 102-5
  *Being and Nothingness* 11; 103
Simons, Margaret 13
Smith, J.Z. 25
Surin, Jean Joseph 28; 68-9

Taves, Anne 33
Teresa of Avila 22; 86-8
Tertullian 88
Tidd, Ursula 21; 92

Weil, Simone 18; 79

# Index of Subjects

absolute 14–18; 29–88; 98–109; 112–13; 118–21
ambiguity 10; 19; 27; 45; 49; 53; 64; 65; 70; 77; 83; 91; 103–22
appeal 15; 27; 30; 39; 43; 72; 84–123
atheism 6; 22; 66; 71–2
auto-immunity 67; 108; 114

being 28–35; 41; 56; 67; 70; 77–112; 122
bourgeoisie 8; 15; 62

capitalism 23; 15; 24; 31–9; 46; 116–17
Christianity 21; 31–42; 106
    Roman Catholic church 6–7; 14–15; 21–2; 60–83; 111; 114; 120
contingency 52; 83; 119–21
consciousness 17–18; 27–9; 47; 55; 75–120

deconstruction 21; 27–30
desire 17; 29; 40–42; 53; 55–87; 91; 104–21; see also – passion
devotion 95–6
dialectic 20–1; 27; 47; 55; 85–9; 93; 105
*différance* 19; 28–30; 35, n. 26; 118

epistemology 19
ethics 14, n. 30; 71; 84; 90; 95; 101–15
evil 29, n. 13; 107–8; 118; 121
existentialism 16; 65–7; 82–5; 102–11

facticity 74; 91–7; 107–11
faith 30; 28–42; 57–68; 72–100
freedom 17; 42; 60–80; 85–113; 116–21

generosity 48; 53; 63; 96; 109

hegemony 15; 25; 34; 38; 55; 66; 114; 117–18
heterology 21; 26
homogeneity 29; 41; 114; 119–19
holiness 38; 67; 119

inheritance 19; 29; 53; 55; 86; 99; 122

joy 72; 75–7; 108
justice 30; 49–50; 76; 84–6; 117–23
justification 90; 93; 99; 104–10

knowledge 27; 30; 38–64; 83; 86; 92; 113–14

Marxism 106
metaphysics 27–39; 48–53; 82; 94; 102–5; 119
mourning 53–7; 82
mysticism 6, n. 2; 14, n. 30; 18–22; 66–71; 77–81

ontology 19; 56; 104
other 4–5; 14–15; 20; 27–67; 71–114

passion 42–8; 56; 69; 74; 104–5; see also – desire
phenomenology 18–19; 85; 104–6
play 3–7; 19; 27; 29; 36; 40; 44; 48; 53; 56; 89–122
project 17–20; 45; 79; 82; 93–122

rapport 86; 100
reciprocity 64; 70; 100; 120
recognition 29; 85; 88–91; 96
religion
   critical theory of 24
   common meaning of 23
   scene of 27–64
response 27; 39–72; 85–91; 105; 109–22
responsibility 19; 28–50; 105–11

sacrifice 37; 42–9; 97; 117–18
salvation 64; 75; 83; 100; 111; 113; 116

self 20; 27–49; 55–67; 83
singularity 27; 39; 41; 43–50; 101; 118–19
solipsism 87; 109–13

totality 29; 35, n. 26; 53; 77–85; 94; 98; 107
transcendence 17–18; 41; 65; 70–83; 90–91

universal 24–5; 30; 33; 44; 49–50; 76; 93–4; 100; 122

violence 31; 34, n. 24; 52, n. 80; 96; 100; 111; 123

www.ingramcontent.com/pod-product-compliance
Lightning Source LLC
Chambersburg PA
CBHW070734230426
43665CB00016B/2233